Imogen Bright Moon creates richly textured, highly tactile woven textile works from yarn that she spins and blends herself. In this elegantly designed book Imogen reveals the secrets of her practice in evocative, engagingly written text accompanied by beautiful samples of her work.

In Chapter One Imogen outlines the different ethical fibres that are available to use, as well as suggesting ways of working with new textures, shades and tones, and ideas for sourcing your own materials. Chapter Two explores different tools and processes for blending, including the historic use of tools, and how you can adapt these into your own studio practice. Next, in Chapter Three, Imogen looks at hand spinning and outlines the different spinners and spindles available while the rest of the book takes you through different finishing techniques, explores how to collect and curate your own yarn collections as well as suggesting different project ideas for a range of different textile crafts.

With an emphasis on engagement with nature, the rhythms of the seasonal craft cycle, ethical making, sustainability and mindfulness, this book is ideal for weavers, textile artists and anyone seduced by the joys of yarn.

Wild Yarn

Wild Yarn

Creating hand-spun yarn from ethical fibres

Imogen Bright Moon

BATSFORD

DEDICATION

This work is dedicated to the craftswomen
who picked up their tools and innovated:
Theo Moorman, Madeleine Vionnet,
Georgia O'Keeffe and Virginia Woolf.

To Clara Nezbah Sherman,
wisdom from Spider Woman:
I offer this work to the First Spinner,
hand to hand, to the very last.

SPINNING

My mother's spindle

is a slender stick

on a hardwood whorl.

Under her fingers

it spins like a dancer,

winding itself

in twisted yarn.

ANN NOLAN CLARK
Little Herder in Autumn

'(The other aspect of) craft work is concerned with art work, the realization of a hope for a lawful and enduring nature. Other elements, such as proportion, space relations, rhythm, predominate in these experiments, as they do in other arts. No limitations other than the veto of the material itself are set. More than an active process, it is a listening for the dictation of the material and a taking in of the laws of harmony. It is for this reason that we can find certitude in the belief that we are taking part in an eternal order.'

ANNI ALBERS
On Designing

Contents

Introduction

What is wild yarn? I have spent eight years finding out, and it's my pleasure to share this journey with you in the pages of this book. It is my hope that you, too, will discover and kindle your experience of yarn through exploring with me, and because I'm a self-taught spinner and weaver, I hope that my 'wild yarn' story will inspire and empower you to spin your own unique yarns for use in your textile practice. Let's begin...

ENCOUNTERING MATERIALS

Whether a proficient spinner or a complete beginner, I believe that each time we encounter our raw materials, it is an opportunity to experience them for the first time. Just as we bring ourselves into the immediate moment of making with whatever our lives contain, the materials are in relationship with us, and we with them. In the arts-therapy model, the raw materials give us permission to be ourselves, just as we are. There is no expectation or idea of perfection from the materials, and nothing they are imposing upon us as a craftsperson.

When I tell people that spinning yarn is forgiving, I mean that the creation of yarn can really hold us with whatever we are holding in ourselves, and the craft itself patiently awaits our encounter to teach us how to be with the process; the rhythm and the 'mistakes' are always a pause to refocus and go deeper. (The same is also true of my main crafts practice of weaving.) Around a quarter of a century ago, Sarah, my then 81-year-old yoga teacher, a former Catholic nun, would say to us at the start of each practice, 'One thing at a time, breathe.' So, with craft, one thing at a time, breathe, becomes one moment of encountering the methods, that turns into a conversation, which becomes your story, breath by breath. Breathe with your materials, breathe with your tools, breathe with your hands: this is the beginning and the end of craft.

CRAFT LANGUAGES

In my earliest woven works, I was attempting to translate the story of the textures and tones of the land, and the mineral forms, shells and knapped flints I was filling my pockets with each time I went to the beach, the woods, or over the South Downs. It was a particular sense of feeling (emotion and texture) that needed to merge to speak the language I was hearing in the landscape. Developing and combining weaving techniques (cloth and tapestry) allowed me tangible access to larger textile spaces of structure and form; however, it was the spinning of yarn, and the haptic processing of raw stuff into a firmer context without losing its essential nature-language, that allowed a way into the authentic translation of the song I was hearing.

I think every artist comes to a place where they can hear the muse communicating, and that might be hard to explain objectively; however, the work created from that conversation, if done with awareness, openness and integrity, has the capacity to hold, echo and broadcast something of these moments of creation. In this way, one's signature, voice, story, and deeply personal process, can be facilitated, supported and amplified through the medium of craft processes and outcomes. I am not seeking to replicate a surface; I am reaching into a bag of raw wool and hoping that I do it justice, that its essence is represented, that I am as light as possible, as gentle in touch and sincere in translation. In this way, the undoing of impactful overdesign, brutal subjugating of materials, denial of Nature herself, is antidoted by works that are as undesigned from a projected imposition, and alchemically distilled into something more real, more ancient and more familiar.

I hope my craft is something that our oldest souls can remember as being their inheritance, to say: *this is old, this is from another time, this is contemporary, this is for me, now...* spinning wild yarn is a deeply connective practice.

1

Sensory Craft

It may seem obvious that craft is a sensory experience, and I would really enjoy exploring why this is important as a creative aspect in itself. Your own body is your primary tool, and from our earliest moments we are sensing and perceiving, via the media of the body, the world we inhabit and the impressions it leaves upon and within our somatic experience. These impressions last a lifetime, and work their way into the psyche-somatic system. Often misrepresented as wholly or partly 'imaginary' in the fields of health (as psychosomatic), the psyche + soma is the unity of the inner experience with the outer physical experience for holistic wellbeing. In the Jungian model, our psyche holds many layers of depth and feeling, both collective and individual; and through craft and the arts, we can give shape and form to these impressions. Through the creation of craft we can speak a language before language, and embody processes to create symbol-forms that powerfully take the place of speech. In this way, craft is a tactile glossary for the senses, and for the soul.

DEFINITIONS

Subtle Comes ultimately from a Latin pair: the prefix *sub-*, meaning 'under,' and *tela*, meaning 'web'. The two were joined in Latin *subtilis*, meaning 'finely woven'. The word was literal; it was originally a weaving term.

Merriam-Webster Dictionary

Subtle matter (n) Rarefied or weightless matter (supposedly) pervading the atmosphere, the universe, the animal body, etc.; a substance of this nature; esp. ether...

Oxford English Dictionary

Layers of Experience

The layers involved in wild-yarn creation as a form of sensory craft might be experienced in the following ways:

OPTIC AESTHETIC The visual texture of yarn – the look, shading, depth, light, shadow. The many shades of naturally coloured wool, the use of botanical plant dyes and inks, and the many ways to use these in harmony or harmonic contrast.

SCENT Wool in all its stages has a depth of scent that often surprises visitors to my exhibitions – not the raw farmyard smell, but the warm, rich comforting scent of wool. Even when washing it in specialist eucalyptus wool soap, the background scent of the essence of wool is beautifully present. Other natural fibres have their own unique scents, and one of my favourites is raw, wild muga silk, when it is warmed. Linen, nettle, jute – all these plant fibres contain scent-memories of the time before they reached my hands.

TOUCH Our hands are involved so thoroughly with the entire crafts process, that we might begin to take these, our earliest tools, for granted. How fibre feels to the touch is incredibly personal, and this can be a very rich point of departure into a new experience of creating wild-yarn.

Under the Web: Considering Tone and Shade

I will be very subtle about the word 'colour', as it implies (in the textile world) the idea that something has been additionally coloured or dyed. Dyeing fibre and yarn is a dedicated craft-form and deserves an entire book in its own right. In this book I will include a set of blended yarn skeins that feature locks (wool curls) that have been traditionally dyed with botanicals, to provide a reference in the discussion of yarn development; however, my own process tends to rarely use dyed fibre, unless it is for a specially requested commission, or something for a theatre production or for a historical museum replica. I will explain my reasons for purposely limiting my use of dyed fibre as you read on, but I encourage you to add in dye work if this calls to your creative vision, and keep it in mind for use in combination with the processes I will be sharing with you. The resource list at the end of the book (see Resources: Fibre & Tool Suppliers) has been compiled to support your research for how best to seek out botanical dyes if you wish to explore them further.

HOW I WORK WITH SHADE AND TONE

Natural wool has its own pigment that constitutes a shade or tone. To me, 'tone' indicates a depth of naturally occurring pigment that produces a 'shade' (a shade of grey, for example). This shade might be blue-ish, or mauve-ish, without actually being the colours blue or purple in a clear, obvious or direct way. Working in what would be perceived as a 'neutral' or 'natural' spectrum of colours is itself a discipline, as it asks us to really look to recognize the nuances between shades, to see how to get the best out of combined shades, and how to use the artistic eye to balance or contrast these tones to blend up a yarn that works for us and our project. Here we get into the similitude I invoke often: *I liken my yarn blending technique to an artist mixing their own paint.* The reason for this is that I have complete control over the blend: I can add light by adding in luminous fibres such as wild silk or seaweed silk; I can mute the tone with a matte plant fibre such as sun-bleached linen; I can add deeper, richer shades of wool to bring the blend into a different colour story. If you enjoy experimental artistic processes and discovering surprising and subtle combinations, then this book is for you!

GENTLE TASK

Consider your relationship with colour, shade, tone, pigment, light and dark. Note which emotions certain shades and tones evoke in you. Do you feel comfortable with a natural-neutral range of shades, or do you prefer botanical dyes? Do you prefer the bright, saturated, vivid colours of an additionally pigmented palette? This is an important step in comprehending your creative needs and finding your artistic voice, using shade and texture to tell a story.

KEY WORDS
light, shine, luminous, gilded, illuminated, reflective, shadow, depth, warmth, richness, resonance.

Texture: Textile, Language and Touch

I will talk a lot about personal signatures in yarn spinning, and in combination with researching the etymological threads of *text-textile-texture*, we can see that *texture* has linguistic roots in describing many forms of artistic expression, from the written and spoken word, the composition and performance of music, and the structure and form of fabric. In my yarn development, texture became the balance to support my exploration of shade and tone. Therefore, my methodology holds 'texture + tone' as an equation I use to fulfill my creative vision, and to which I return when I need to remember the founding principles of my practice.

HOW I WORK WITH TEXTURE

Single-origin fibres each have their unique journey and story. For example, some rare-breed sheep flocks I work with have named sheep that are dear pets, and their age and location yield a diverse variety of textures year-on-year, which are very powerful to use in my creative practice, as the very fibres themselves hold a story. Texture, or the implicit *quality* of the fibre, has its own lexicon: wool may be bulky, lofty, crimped, warm; silk may be smooth, slubbed and scaled; linen, flax and nettle may be firm, dry, cool, crisp.

The textural qualities of each chosen fibre are unique, and how I combine those together has the artistic methodology of an artisan craft; that is, I am creatively attempting to communicate something of my personal vision, my relationship to and with textile, through the medium of my blended and handspun yarn. I'm searching to combine the differing characters of textures that work together, either in balanced contrast or in aesthetic harmony, that begin to form a visual language, and the spin starts to add the signature personal to me – as your spin will be personal to you – and then the story of the textile work I am crafting is on its way to becoming realized in the final project or finished piece of work.

GENTLE TASK

I invite you to consider what your own creative equation might consist of, and keep it in mind as you encounter your yarn work going forwards.

DICTIONARY

Texture (n) The visual or tactile surface characteristics and appearance of something; the disposition or manner of union of the particles of a body or substance; a composite of the elements of prose or poetry; identifying quality: character; something composed of closely interwoven elements, specifically: a woven cloth; the structure formed by the threads of a fabric; basic scheme or structure; overall structure.

Texture (v) To give a particular texture to.

Merriam-Webster Dictionary

Texture (n) The process or art of weaving. Obsolete.

Texture (v) To construct by or as by weaving; to give a texture to (anything).

Oxford English Dictionary

Here, in the space of actively working with texture, my practice becomes more practically considered and tactile: whereas the shade-tone process can be more imaginal and visionary, the texture process requires hands-on experiential and tangible moments to understand the characteristic qualities of the fibres I'm selecting. This is where having time to explore and gather samples of fibres that speak to you as a spinner is really key. Fibre can be gathered from a range of sources to allow a set of sample yarns to be blended and spun. Once texture becomes a focus of yarn development, and fibre research is underway, another significant aspect of craft ethics comes into play: the ethical sourcing of fibres.

GENTLE TASK

Feel into which textures amplify your emotions. Note the textures you perceive as smooth, airy, cool, firm, tight, soft, lofty, dense, substantial, weighty. Create an artistic equation that will support your creative spinning practice. Begin researching fibres, and deeply consider your personal ethics and how these can support your approach to sourcing the right fibres for you.

NATURE AS CREATIVE PARTNER

It all begins with the weather. Your local area will yield fibres that are suitable for your environment. The microclimate we inhabit, along with its weather fronts, is also home to plants and creatures that are adapted to live alongside us, or rather, if we are being good ancestors, that we should strive to live harmoniously alongside.

When I first encountered the rescue flock from the Sheep Ahoy Animal Rescue charity based in Kent in the spring of 2017, it struck me that the fleece was telling me the story of the land. They are mainly Southdown sheep, perfectly woollen to cope with the mist and cool damp mornings of the South Downs, a range of chalk hills in the south-eastern coastal counties of England. The bowl of the chalk downs hosts a microclimate of warmth, specifically in Brighton, and in pockets along the south-east coastline. This fleece, then, was site specific, a distillation of the land and the needs of the weather. Southdown sheep fleece is short and body-full, close to the body of the sheep and tightly crimped to create a barrier from the salty mist, yet not long enough for overheating in the warmer spring and autumn, pre-and-post shear, which is usually May (April if it is particularly warm and there is a limited risk of a cold snap). The secondary additions to the flock were sheep from the Romney Marshes, low-ground up the coast to the east that is wetter and more saturated. The damp conditions call for a longer fleece with different qualities: the longer fleece drips, it allows damp to condense and roll off, and the sheep becomes a cloud.

'we must come down to earth from the clouds where we live in vagueness, and experience the most real thing there is: material... Material, that is to say unformed and unshaped matter...'

ANNI ALBERS
On Designing

KEY WORDS
touch, haptic, tactile,
sensory, tangible.

What the sheep are grazing on in their local environment is also key. The rare-breed North Ronaldsay flock on the Isle of Auskerry, a small island in eastern Orkney, Scotland, only eat the seaweed on their rocky shore, and this has created one of the most mythic fleeces I've had the pleasure to work with. The sheep appear to be moving rocks, their shading identical to their landscape. The iodine-rich fleece is soft and strong, perfectly adapted to island life, with a double coat of fibres of differing qualities. This sheep breed still (partially) holds on to its ancient method of self-shedding, something that has been outbred from many other flocks that require shearing interventions.

ANIMAL WELFARE

Many people are becoming more aware of our relationship with animals and the wider natural world, and I'm often asked about potential conflicts of feeling and my own ethical approach to using wool and fibre-yielding animal products, including wild harvested silk (also known as peace silk). My position is one of mindfulness and of educating myself around animal welfare, saving fleece from being wasted, and choosing suppliers who have holistic, integrative and regenerative relationships with the natural world and precious resources. (Many people don't realize how non-peace silk fibre is obtained, for example, so I'll cover that in more detail when we discuss types of fibre for spinning in Chapter Three: Spinning Beauty.)

Sourcing Ethical Fibres

The first sacks of wool that I was completely responsible for processing were sheared from the Sheep Ahoy rescue flock, which is comprised of 75 per cent Southdown and 25 per cent Romney Marsh sheep. This small flock is cared for by Julia, a proud vegan activist who actively identifies and rescues sheep from livestock auctions, saving them from haulage from the UK on to the Continent. The sheep she selects should not have been put into auction (reasons vary from the size of the sheep to their wellness and condition), and often Julia's intervention is enough for the sheep to be delivered into her care, to live their future life in a field as a loved pet with all the healthcare and attention they need.

I felt a huge duty of care and responsibility to process my first-ever direct resource as ethically as possible, therefore I was able to use the services of The Natural Fibre Company to clean, scour and card my sacks of wool to an organic standard. Two seasons of working with Sheep Ahoy and The Natural Fibre Company (2017 and 2018) has provided me with traceable, ethical, local wool for the foreseeable future.

Other wool I source comes from a spectrum of mindful and ethically responsible suppliers. The Isle of Auskerry has a 700-strong flock of rare-breed North Ronaldsay sheep that are tended and sheared by Teresa Probert and her family, who use the traditional method of shearing by hand with metal shears to assist the natural self-shedding process of this breed. Lauriston Farm, a biodynamic social-farming business on the Blackwater Estuary in rural Essex, has a flock of North Ronaldsay sheep and they produce their own yarns. Biodynamic gardening and animal care are becoming better known, and I'd encourage everyone who works with fibre to look into it as a process and holistic practice, from growing fleece to cultivating dye plants.

Fernhill Fibre, located in the Mendip Hills in Somerset, has a regenerative flock of sheep with variegated fleeces in many shades, and they offer whole fleeces for sale during shearing season. This is a lovely way to spin a single-origin yarn from one sheep at a time. As the supply is small and varies each year, it's good to buy what you need to get you through your spinning projects until the next year's shear. Hampshire Wood Projects generously gifted me a huge supply of their domestic Huacaya alpaca hair, which is oil-free and exceptionally soft. I've also been commissioned in the past to spin the beautifully soft hair of a Tibetan mastiff named Vajra that had the texture and shade qualities of a finely powdered charcoal smoke cloud.

ASK YOUR WEB

It's amazing how many people have access to, or know of, people with a sheep or two, or indeed a whole flock, where the wool is sheared and composted. The reasons for wool being 'wasted' or used for things other than yarn-making (roof insulation, for example) is that it often costs more to shear the fleece than it can be sold for through an organization such as British Wool (formerly the British Wool Marketing Board). This conundrum leaves a lot of small-flock owners to give up on producing wool for sale, and instead it is burnt, dug into the ground, used as mulch, or thrown away (or sometimes it can be collected by insulation producers). It seems such a huge loss when these are animals that we have bred to need shearing (the original sheep breeds of antiquity shed their own fleece naturally, as some of the North Ronaldsay sheep are still able to do). With historical agricultural progress, animal husbandry bred 'better' wool for textiles, and that wool needed human intervention to be sheared on an annual or biannual basis, and this is the situation we are in today: we are responsible for the care of animals that have been bred for shearing, so making use of that fleece, in my ethos, honours the animal and respects its produce.

GATHERING WAYSIDE PLANTS

Depending on your location, it may be possible to forage (or grow and harvest) your own plant fibres. As Allan Brown and Dylan Howitt show us in their beautiful film *The Nettle Dress*, it is possible to visit a woodland (or wasteland) and harvest enough wild nettles to spin and weave a dress. This is slow craft in real time: seven years of growth, gathering, life, death, spinning. *The Nettle Dress* sets us the example of craft as a real and essential part of life, as a helper to our human experience, and as an outcome of many processes and many downpours, as well as those moments of utter luminous joy.

GENTLE TASK

Begin with searching out your yarn fibres. Look locally. Get into a relationship with the land and the fibre. Start your yarn-story of discovery, of up-skilling, and adapting to what is available.

KEY WORDS

land, local, soil, nutrition, welfare, growth, harvest, process, sustainability, forage, rewilding.

Seeking Inspiration

Open yourself to the muse. Inspiration and one's connection to artistic flow is deeply personal, and it comes easily to some and needs more encouragement for others. Take some time to check in with your creativity and listen for what you need to best support yourself, and build that into your crafts practice. Find inspiration in your world, dreams, symbols, your cultural heritages and your lived experiences, folk stories and music, that support you where you are and provide food for the muse.

GENTLE TASK

Regard nature, witness the weather, go for a journey into local wild spaces, connect with your senses. Begin imagining your textile-languages of texture, shade and tone; start a dedicated wild-yarn notebook to support your crafts practice as you read this book.

FIBRE TYPES TO RESEARCH

Seek out the folk stories and mythologies of regional fibres; investigate the historical methodologies, specialist tools and heritage applications to get a full-spectrum picture of why these fibres became (or are becoming) part of our human story of textiles:

WOOL Sheep
HAIR Camel, yak, goat, rabbit, dog
BAST Flax, linen, lime, hemp, nettle
BUD Cotton

DICTIONARY

Pearl An organic mollusk-derived substance, having a composition of 86% calcium carbonate, 10% conchiolin (conch = shell of the sea snail), with remining elements up to 4% is constituted of water. **Conchiolin** is a protein which forms a matrix, upon which the shell is built from calcium carbonate, (notes from Banfield & Cook-Wallace, *Pearls and Other Organic Gems*).

conchiolin (n) A scleroprotein forming the organic basis of mollusk shells (as mother-of-pearl)

Merriam-Webster Dictionary

ADDITIONAL FIBRE NOTES

PROTEIN Fibres can be created from the casein derived from milk, for example, to create a soft fibre known as milk cotton.

SILK Peace silks or wild silks are harvested without requiring the death of the silk moth, which is not the case in traditional silk processing. These silks are naturally pigmented depending on the diet of the silk moth: eri silk is naturally orange from castor plants, and muga silk from a combination of laurel and cinnamon trees from the magnolia family; tussar (tussah) silk is a very pale gold as the moth feeds on the Indian almond tree, and the naturally pewter-grey peduncle silk is named from its role as a suspending fibre for the tussar silk cocoon.

CELLULOSE Best known are rayon and viscose, but in more recent years, a world of silk-like fibres has been created that have those same qualities of being light-giving and dyeable. These new fibres are created from organic matter such as plants and cellulose-based algae, including soy, mint, rose, seaweed (SeaCell), corn silk, and eucalyptus cellulose infused with powdered pearl. These fibres, while being plant derived, employ a lot of chemical processes in their creation; therefore, I would encourage you to research their farming and production methods further to determine your own response to them.

KEY WORDS

quietude, peace, embodiment, therapeutic, calm, natural crafts, heritage, culture, antiquity, symbols, dreams, folk tales.

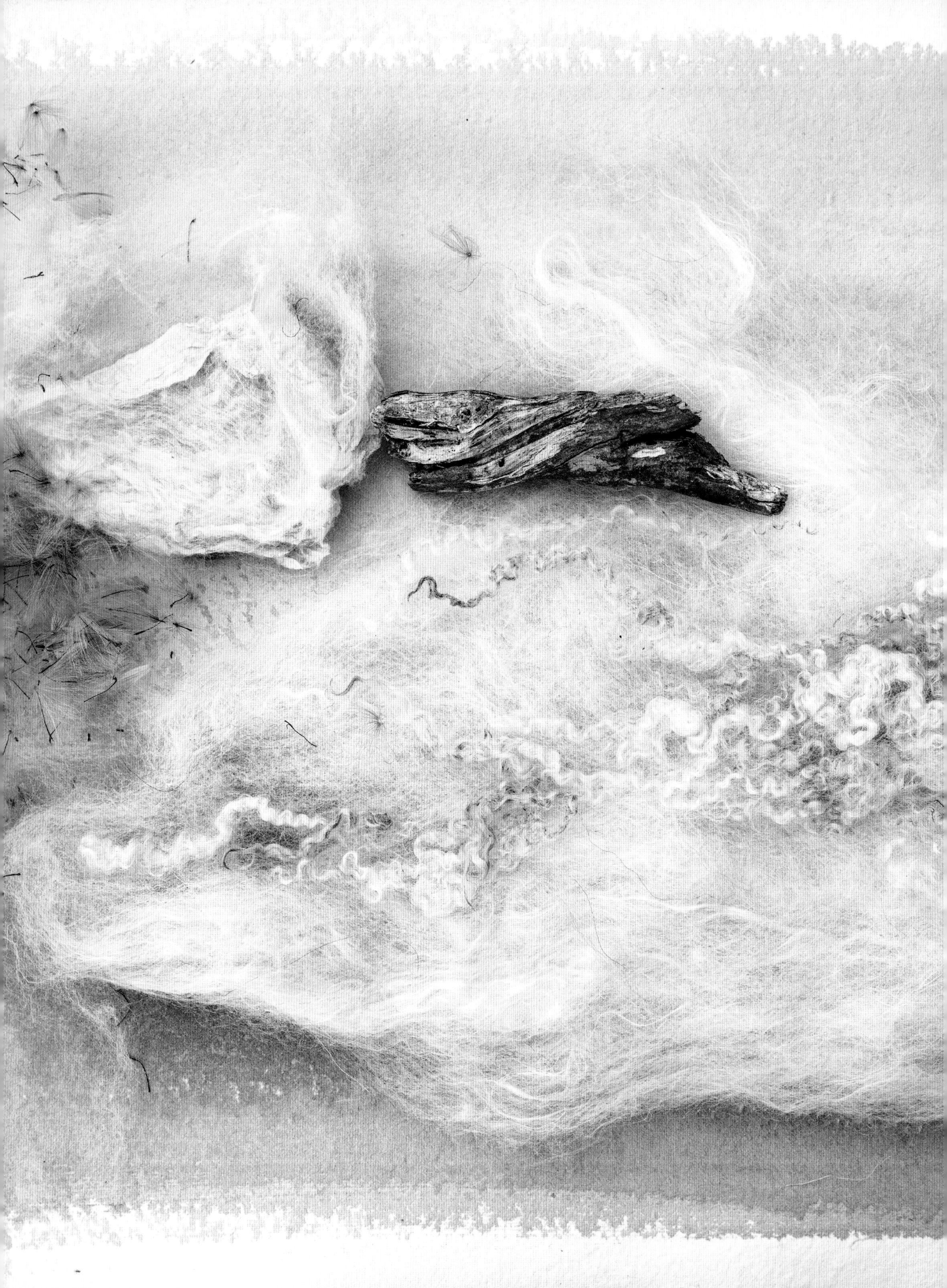

2

Painting with Wool

This chapter will be an exploration of tools and processes, looking at the historical use of tools and how you can adapt them into your studio practice today. It is also an invitation to reconsider tools from their original context and purpose, to explore how, for example, wool combs, carders, hackles and our own hands can find a new way of blending wool that might break some old rules and create some new improvisation, leading to new developments in yarn creation.

'the voluptuous beauty of unwoven yarns, of unspun fleece, silk, flax, tow and jute…can contribute to works of immense richness, depth, and lasting value…'

THEO MOORMAN,
Weaving as an Art Form

'I have picked flowers where I found them –
have picked up sea shells and rocks and pieces of
wood where there were sea shells and rocks and
pieces of wood that I liked.
When I found beautiful white bones on the
desert I picked them up and took them home too.
I have used these things to say what is to me the
wideness and wonder of the world as I live in it.'

GEORGIA O'KEEFFE,
Some Memories of Drawings

Blend Inspiration: Landscape, Texture and Feeling

Extracting the essence of natural materials into a texture-tone language for yarn blending is deeply personal and yet it is also a collective experience: to have these beautiful materials around us in our shared world, and to encounter and translate our own personal relationship through crafted works, and to then reflect and share those impressions back out into the world. This is the creative prerogative and gift of the artist, and it is the essence of archetypal symbolism: a rock is a rock, is our rock, is our conversation and expression with and of, and through, the medium (of yarn).

In this way, yarn blending can become a crafted diary: days of the year represented in the seasons of materials; the how and why and when of their discovery; the record keeping of their meaning in our lives. The yarns spun from these sources of inspiration form the ground for the traditional *sampler* in textile traditions: I am weaving the weather; I am spinning a stone.

Researching historic and heritage wool-processing techniques is incredibly rewarding. We can chart the passage of time, the changes in fortunes and the progress of economic interventions through the working of yarns and the creation of textile. Some of this history is challenging and difficult, and it takes time for us to meet certain methods with the understanding of a deep and complicated journey today.

KEY WORDS

feather, shell, stone, chalk, mineral, bark, tilth, earth, seed, husk, tuft, down, root, rock, wood, web, nacre, moss, kelp, drift, vine, cloud, dew, pollen, puddle, ice, rain, river, clay...

My Studio Tools

Certain advances in technology, similar to the sewing machine, have allowed adaptations into small-scale studio wool-processing, whereby motorized drum carders (and electric spinning wheels) are now affordable and popular. Here, I will outline my use of tools and why and for which purposes I use them. I will also discuss the advantages of analogue tools which is two-fold: simplicity of use and economy of running.

To be very practical, if we lost the ability to run electricity in the studio, how would we continue to create? If there was a power cut, or if the cost of running equipment became too high (as it did in 2022-2023), how easy would it be to switch back to hand tools? How would this affect the yarn creation: would it look drastically different, or would it yield significantly less yarn?
As a craftsperson, how would I cope creatively with this adjustment?

Before we answer these questions, I'd like to share my tool timeline and some definitions, which shows some adaptations and integrations I have had to make when things are in flux:

2016 Hand carders

2017 Small manual drum carder (Wingham, 25g/1oz batts per full drum)

2018 Wool combs and double-row hackle

2019 Large motorized drum carder (Strauch, 100g/4oz batts per full drum)

2022 Blending board

2023 Wide manual drum carder with handle adaptation (Wingham, 75g/3oz batts per full drum)

2024 Combination of all tools as needed

DEFINITIONS

Rolags These are the produce of hand–carders, whereby the carded fibred is lifted, peeled and rolled off the surface of the carding paddle, creating a tube–like structure of fibres that are ready to spin from the edge. Rolags can be effectively made on a blending board where the depth of the fibre packing is shallow or layered using delicate fibres such as silk. These types of blends can be eased off the carders or board with the assistance of wooden dowels, which can be used to pull and roll in sections to create more delicate rolags.

Batts These are created on a larger surface such as a blending board or drum carder and can be more densely packed by means of brushes to impact the fibres on the surface of these tools. Batts are removes (made to be removed) like rolags, so are made by lifting, peeling and rolling the batt off the surface of the board or drum. Batts can then be stored flat and spun from the corner or pulled into horizontal segments to spin. Batts can also be rolled up and spun from the edge, in the same way as the smaller rolag.

Almost all of my wool-blending tools are manual, requiring no power supply, save myself! The exception is the motorized drum carder and in 2022 I packed this important piece of equipment away, primarily due to the rising fuel costs, and additionally because I wanted to take the opportunity to assess my own practice and relationship to my tools, to see if combining new ways of working would bring me back into alignment with my original wild-yarn vision of textured and characterful yarns.

ERGONOMICS AND TAKING CARE OF YOUR BODY

From 2016-2019 I was exclusively hand processing my wool ready for spinning, and my body had something to say about it! Long hours using the hand carders, and then the manual drum carder, created some discomfort and RSI (repetitive strain injury) in my wrist, shoulder and elbow, which I managed by switching tasks frequently – for example, carding then spinning in small batches. However, it was my friend-in-craft Tom van Deijnen (also known as Tom of Holland) who said perhaps it was time to look at a motorized drum carder, as I was spending more time on the blending process for my woven works. This is, of course, an important moment for any craftsperson, when they need to face the conundrum of productivity, the idea that: If I amplify one process and create 'more', but it negatively impacts my body, should I make less? Or should I invite some industrial progress into my tools, with the additional costs and implications?

Here's how I adapted to meet my needs at that time. Before making a purchase, I looked at other ways to blend yarn, and helpfully I was lent a few tools by fellow makers to experiment with, to see if they worked for my needs.

Wool Combs and Hackles

The English wool combs, as revived by Peter Teal in his 1970s book *Hand Woolcombing and Spinning*, allow for a different set of movements based on the combing of raw or washed fleece that is in its cut-state, whereby it is clear to see the clip and the tip. This allows the locks to be aligned on the combs and, with a circular motion, to comb the wool into a lustrous and static-infused cloud (the static build up can be remedied by having a water spray bottle close to hand with a few drops of lavender oil added). The original English wool combs and the newer, lighter editions can feature either a single or a double row of tines, allowing for the processing of different fibre lengths, and for separating fleece that has a long top fleece and a shorter underwool. The tines are incredibly sharp and the technique involves wielding the comb in a circle, therefore they need to be used with care in a suitable safe space. Some editions of the English wool combs can be mounted and clamped to a worktop; others you can use in the hand as with hand carders.

There is something very dynamic about working a fleece on the wool combs, and its intended purpose as a tool to align the fibres in the same direction is the historic method that allows the spinning of worsted wool, which produces a firm and tight spin suitable for suiting and tweeds.

When we discuss spinning in the following chapters, it's helpful to think of traditionally *worsted* fibre preparation as cloth yarn that is woven, and *woollen* prepared yarn as loftier and more air-filled, for knitting and creating fabrics with a greater degree of bulky softness. There is also an implication with traditional spin direction, which again will be discussed later. Here, I am tracking the process of these methods; however, I fully intend to improvise and mix methods, thus lending a variety of techniques into the development of wild yarn.

Hackles , like the one shown left, are traditionally used for flax linen and bast plant fibres, which require a few processes to ret (rot), skutch (scrape) and break down the outer shell of the plant to reveal the long fibres within. The hackles are used to draw the fibres through with a circular motion, and with each pass the hank of linen becomes finer and finer, adding shine and smoothness, ready to dress a distaff* for spinning. Working linen on a hackle has a similar affinity of motion to the wool combs, and contemporary hackles can be sourced with single and double tine rows and give a wide working area. The hackle I use is clamped to the edge of my workbench with G-clamps and makes for a versatile addition to the studio.

***A distaff is a wooden pole used to arrange and mount fibre (usually linen) ready for orderly spinning. St Distaff's Day falls on the 7th January and it is a medieval folk tradition heralding the first day of spinning after the festivities of Twelfth Night/Epiphany.**

USING THE HACKLE AND ENGLISH WOOL COMB

As you may sense, I'm not a traditionalist. In as much as I respect the historical context these tools were originally created and intended for, I also see the potential in experimenting and improvising to create a new methodology. Because I mix fibres as I blend, sometimes I pre-comb, card or hackle a small amount of fibre by hand, and I then add this into a larger blend. When I'm using the hackle, I can load up the full width of the hackle by adding in layers and 'moments' of variegated fibres to build up a blend that can be seen growing vertically. To this I can add fibres in various states of texture and process, adding very smooth pre-carded fibres in with uncombed fleece, silk, linen, etc.

There are three ways to remove the final blend from the hackle:

METHOD ONE Use a wool comb to comb through the stacked yarn. This blends and removes large sections of fibre that can be set aside to spin as a cloud, or further put through a drum carder to add an extra blend and make the variegation less pronounced.

METHOD TWO Use a diz, a flat or curved button-like tool (made from horn or wood) with various sized holes, to allow you to pull the fibre off a hackle or comb into a roving sliver of a consistent width for spinning (see image on page 33).

METHOD THREE Use your hands to extract the fibre into a sliver of variegated width. The first pulls are the most consistent; the closer you get to the tines, the shorter and more compact the fibres will be, and these may need to be lifted off and worked by hand to get them into a suitable form for spinning.

If you are feeling suitably emboldened, you can always spin straight off the hackle and see what happens. Sometimes saving time in processing allows for new processes to reveal themselves, and therefore creates new outcomes.

USING HAND CARDERS AND BLENDING BOARDS

Hand carders are usually the first technique encountered in yarn work and fibre processing; paddle carders come in pairs with affixed tine-cloth, the red version and the blue, which has finer tines for carding out finer rolags. Rolags can be rolled and lifted off the carder and set aside, ready for spinning. Alternatively, you can lift a batt off the surface of the carder and set it aside and spin from the batt without rolling it up (more on this technique later).

Blending boards, like the one shown right, are a really wonderful intermediary tool between a hand carder and a drum carder. Using the same tine-cloth seen on the paddle carders, affixed to ply board with upholstery staples, this creates what is effectively a large carding panel that can sit on a tabletop or on the lap. There are pre-made versions available from tool suppliers such as Wingham Wool Work and Ashford (see Resources: fibre and tool supplier), however I decided to make my own as an experiment (see page 44 for instructions).

Making and Using a Simple Blending Board

YOU WILL NEED

- A3 plywood drawing board – if it comes with a stand to allow a slope this is a benefit as it offers you a choice of positions
- Tine cloth – this can be purchased off a roll and is 30cm (12in) wide as standard; a 30cm (12in) square fits nicely onto an A3 drawing board
- Pliers – for removing any tines should you need to trim the cloth
- Upholstery staple gun and staples
- Circular wooden body brush – preferably with a hand strap to allow your hand to be flat in the blending technique
- Small or standard hand carder – to remove the finished blend
- Pair of 50cm (20in) wooden dowels – for alternative removal method (optional)

METHOD

Staple the edges of the tine cloth to the plywood, ensuring it is flat and even by alternating stapling between parallel sides as you go – left and right sides first, then upper and lower edges.

USE

My method is very simple. I pull strands of fibre down through the tines, building up a layer across the surface. Once there is good coverage for my needs, I use the body brush to pack down the fibre using minimal downward strokes. Choosing a body brush with a hand strap allows the hand to take a relaxed position and apply even pressure.

Continue adding and packing layers in this way until the depth of the tines is filled. Now use the carder to gently flick up the lower edge to allow the batt to be fully peeled off the blending board. As an alternative, place one dowel in front and one behind the batt to lift and gently roll it off the board, a method I've seen used effectively for finely blended yarns, often with vibrant colourways, but I don't find this technique works for the consistency of texture I'm looking for.

This gives you a really good medium-sized batt that can be lightly rolled or laid flat ready for spinning. When handling blended batts, keep the air between layers nice and spongy: avoid forceful compression or overhandling, and layer between tissue paper if necessary.

Note: If you use felting in your crafts practice, a thin layer of fibre blended in this way gives an excellent outer layer to a felted base. For inspirational felt artists, please research the works of Gladys Paulus, Yuli Somme and Moira Bateman.

Drum Carders

Drum carders offer the opportunity to create batches of batts in a more time-effective way, either by hand with a crank handle (manual drum carder) or by machine with a motor similar to that on an industrial sewing machine (motorized drum carder). Let's look at the considerations for each in turn.

MANUAL DRUM CARDER

This is a really easy tool to use that can be set up on a kitchen table or in a workshop, by affixing it to the edge of a worktop with clamps so that the crank handle is free to rotate along the edge of the work surface. Bear in mind that the handles may be set up for right-handed makers, so you may need to ask for a modification if you prefer a left-handed handle. It is also worth noting that there are some makes that have the option for an adapted crank handle that requires fewer turns with greater leverage.

The handle rotates the drums (one large and one smaller) by means of a drive band and cogs, and, technically, it is similar to either a sewing machine or a spinning wheel. As a person-powered tool, the dominant arm you will be using will definitely feel the effects. I would recommend building up to longer shifts as your muscles may not become uncomfortable until the following day. It is easy to spend hours at a time carding only to be in great discomfort for days after, so please take notice of what your body needs and what it is telling you. (The same applies to hand carders and wool combs, although the hackle and blending board are more ergonomically sensitive and I've found both to be good antidotes to other forms of manual carding.)

MOTORIZED DRUM CARDER

If you find yourself ever-increasingly blending for your yarn practice, then it might be the moment to invest in a motorized drum carder. This is an industrial machine and needs to be safely housed in a workshop (ideally lockable), to be kept out of reach of children and pets. The safety implications are very important: on my model, the lower carding drum consists of tiny knives rather than pin-tines, and the weight, force and speed of a motorized drum carder requires the usual safety precautions of any mechanical workshop.

- Tie hair back and remove long necklaces and any hazardous jewellery.
- *Do not* wear clothing with long or loose sleeves; *do* wear flat safety footwear.
- Check you are fit for work: some medications are contraindicated for the use of machinery.
- No drinks near the machinery!
- Ensure a safe industrial plug, and always switch off and unplug from the wall when not in use.
- Practise an emergency-break sequence with the power supply and off switch.
- Understand the rhythm of the machine and how to control the speed dials and the drum balance.
- Familiarize yourself with some technical mechanics: oiling moving parts, cleaning out debris, checking chain tension, checking basic electrics, always switching off the power supply at the wall and unplugging first, but if in any doubt, please consult a registered tradesperson.

Motorized drum carders come in a variety of widths and are made by several well-respected brands. For my purposes, to create highly textured batts, I wanted the largest drum available to me that would use my budget effectively, so I invested in a Strauch Mad Batt'r, which was built in the USA and imported over to my studio. I've used it a great deal in the past four years, and I've also stored it away at times, either during a studio move or because of the cost of powering it. It's currently back up and running, and ready whenever I need to use it.

BLENDING ON A MANUAL AND MOTORIZED DRUM CARDER

This is best understood by explaining the elements of a drum carder:

LICKER-IN DRUM This is the smaller drum, set to the front of the carder, which catches the fibre you place in front of it and delivers it onto the larger main drum. The licker-in drum usually has the same tine cloth as the main drum; however, on some motorized drum carders, this drum has small blades instead of tines. The licker-in drum is adjustable and can be moved closer to or further away from the main drum, depending on the thickness of the fibres you are carding; for example, silk and linen would need a closer setting, whereas locks and bulky raw wool require a wider, more open setting. I tend to blend finer fibres such as silk and linen into my wool, and often my wool is scoured raw fleece, which is chunky and bulky, so I set a mid-open space between my drums, so as not to jam and jar them with the bulk of the fleece.

MAIN DRUM The larger drum collects and aligns the fibres into a batt, and with each turn of the crank handle you are carding and aligning your fibres into your preferred spinning texture. It also acts as a 'paint drum', allowing you to build up layers of tone and shade to inform your final yarn. Depending on the size of your main drum, you can expect a full batt to be anywhere from 25g to 100g (1oz to 4oz).

DRIVE BAND AND WHEELS A set of wheels or cogs and the strong band that together turn both wheels as you crank the handle. Motorized carders usually have metal-toothed cogs and metal chains (like a bike chain), while manual versions have synthetic bands or belts, usually made from polycord or polyurethane.

PACKING BRUSH This looks a lot like a dog brush and is used to compress or 'pack down' the fibre as its added to the drum, to get a more cohesive batt and make best use of the surface area of the drum.

DOFFER SPIKE OR HOOK This metal hooked tool should be run along the wooden guide to enable you to remove the batt from the carder.

SMALL CARDING BRUSH To assist in combing off the batt from the drum.

CRANK HANDLE The crank handle on a manual drum carder turns the main (large) drum clockwise or anticlockwise, as you control the direction: forwards, to card fibres onto the drum; backwards, to remove the batt from the drum.

Pre-preparation of Fibres: in the Grease, or Not in the Grease?

If you are intending to blend into a base of raw scoured wool (i.e. wool that has been supplied straight from the sheep and cleaned), this should be soaked, scoured then dried, and be clean enough to handle. Exceptionally raw wool will contain dirt, vegetable matter and, of course, animal droppings, as well as *suint*, a type of crystallized grease at the roots of the clip, which is not the same as the moisturizing lanolin wax that is good for spinning. Knowing the difference between dirty and lanolin-rich '*greasy*' wool is important. For the past few years, The Guild of Spinners, Weavers and Dyers has been encouraging an open conversation about spinning with raw wool, wool in the grease and scoured wool. I'll offer my insights here based on my experiences of cleaning raw 'sheep fresh' fleece – wool that has been clipped, rolled and delivered straight from the animal.

Sometimes raw fleece has been 'skirted', meaning the muddiest and filthiest areas closest to the floor and the back end of the animal have been removed, and some of the more obvious dirt has been pulled out. With the right attitude it is possible to salvage most dirty wool if one is prepared for the hard work of cleaning it. Raw fleece needs to be cleaned or used within a year or two of storage due to the potential for maggots (sorry!).

Safety note: Raw-state fleece is a hazard for pregnant women due to the risk of listeria. Always wear gloves to protect yourself from contact with the dirtiest matter.

RAINWATER SOAK Once I receive any raw fleece, I put it into a rainwater soak tub for a few days (I use large builders' rubble buckets with handles, covered with netting for safety). This is out of the house and near a main drain that I can pour the soak water into, although as this soak doesn't use soap, the water would also be suitable for putting onto plants. This soak encourages any dust, surface dirt, seeds and other vegetable matter to loosen and sink to the bottom of the bucket. It also encourages the fibres to open up and push out any dirt.

AIR-DRY I dry out the rainwater-soaked fleece on drying racks and shelves, by turning it in a warm space – outside on a sunny day, or in a garage or conservatory with good sunlight and some background warmth on cooler days. It's important to get the fleece dried out within two to three days so that it doesn't mildew or start to smell musty. Once it has air-dried, you can assess the cleanliness and quality, and see more of the natural body and texture of the wool.

ASSESSMENT At this stage, the wool is as dirt-free as you can achieve with cold water alone, and it will have lost none of its natural grease. If the wool looks and feels workable, use your judgement. Sample some with the hand carders: if it feels nicely oily and looks fresh, then this is fine to card and potentially spin straight from the fleece. If, however, it is discoloured with soil (more obvious in white wool), full of suint (which can look like white-yellow resin or crystalline grease), or needs a bit more attention, then the next step is to scour the wool.

SCOUR For this, you will need hot water and a degreasing agent, such as a liquid soap formulated to deep-clean greasy wool. Some products are harsher than others, but it is possible to scour the wool without fully stripping the natural oils (i.e. lanolin) beneficial for the condition of the wool and the spin. Choose a product that contains natural oils known for their cleaning properties, such as eucalyptus, citrus and lavender. Fill a large tub with hand-hot water (the heat of the hottest bath) adding in the liquid soap, then gently lay the fleece over the whole area of the surface of the water, so that the water is absorbed into the fleece, naturally pulling the wool into the water. You may want to gently push down or use a stick to get the wool as submerged as possible, all the time *not* agitating the wool. The trick to scouring wool is to only soak it, not 'wash' or scrub it, as heat + soap + wool = felt! Allow the scouring-soak process to take some time, perhaps a few hours, and once the water is cooling, the suint-grease removal will have taken effect (heat is needed to dissolve the greasy-waxy crystals). Push the fleece to one side (or lift it out of the tub) and drain the dirty water; if the drained water is particularly muddy, repeat the scouring process until you are satisfied that the runoff water is as clean as possible (the yarn will be washed again after spinning, so there is a tolerance here with what you find personally acceptable to continue with the next steps in the process).

AIR-DRY (AGAIN) As before, air-dry your scoured fleece on drying racks or shelves, turning regularly and ensuring the centre of the fibres are drying out in good time (within a few days to avoid becoming musty). Once a fleece is fully cleaned and completely dried, it can be stored well for years before being used.

SEPARATING FIBRES This is a good opportunity to assess the fibres of the fleece by pulling them apart and separating them by hand, to give you an idea of the way you want to work with it. Does it have a quality that you want to capture and not overprocess? Do you want to card it and see how it behaves? Now that you can see the true colour, what other shades will it tone well with? Which textures could you include in a blend to accompany it? This is where the wool starts to let you know what it needs.

STORAGE Wool should be stored well to avoid moth attacks. Plastic is obviously mothproof, but it can sweat the wool and create condensation, which risks mildew. Compostable bioplastic is not suitable for wool storage as it will degrade on to the wool. I've had success with storing fleece in heavy-duty paper potato sacks which can be sealed, and I also use large calico laundry sacks which provide air-flow and are so far holding up very well. Howsoever you choose to store your wool, check on it regularly and circulate the storage, making sure it is dry and the conditions are ambient (an attic, tanked basement or insulated garage is great).

By separating whole fleeces into smaller sacks, it is possible, if moths are suspected, to rescue bags by putting them into cold storage (a chest freezer) for 10-14 days, before re-scouring. Or, if a summer infestation of wool moth is caught early, then those bags can be removed and disposed of to protect the rest of the batch – wool makes an excellent mulch for growing plants, so compost can be its final use. Sometimes wool doesn't make it through storage. That's life. Therefore it is wise to buy only what you know you will be using for the next year or two, storing it as well as possible.

The Process of Painterly Blending

Now you are acquainted with the tools and the wool preparation methods, it's time to begin blending. Whichever set of tools you use, the basic methodology and principles of blending remain the same, and I shall lay these out for you here. Begin with a principal selection of three fibres that have the potential to work together to manifest the yarn from your inspirational reference material (feather, stone, shell, etc.). Here, we may borrow terms from the perfumer's craft: a base note, heart and top note.

THE BASE This gives *depth* to the ground and the underlying strength to the whole texture study, and depending on your selection, this might be chalky, silken, lustrous, full of kemp, roughly carded, or a completely refined and aligned fibre. It should capture the essence of what you are conveying.

THE HEART This gives *body and tone* to the whole by amplifying the qualities of the base, and at the same time either complementing the shade (*harmony*) or contrasting the shade (known in yarn work as *humbug*). This is the space to be especially subtle, if opportunity allows: to combine fibres that are perhaps a slight tone-shift apart, or bring out the underlying redness in a black fibre, or the mauve-ish quality of a grey fibre. This is where I look to add something of the bridge that will balance the work and create narrative cohesion. Equally, if I am seeking a harmonious contrast, I would still be looking to complement the base texture, but with a humbug (contrasting) shade; for example, a matte cream base with a deep matte grey complement. There should be meaningful contrast that works together in the aesthetic. I would also include fibres here such as flax, nettle and hemp, as these are texture-giving fibres, meaning they add body. Fibre choices such as mohair and alpaca work well here also, as they have their own specific texture qualities that can be added into the base to a lesser or greater degree, depending on how much they support your vision.

THE TOP This is the space of adding *lustre and light* with specialist fibres to add an upper note of luminosity, gilding or reflectivity. This is usually a rare-fibre addition, used sparingly and with care to amplify its effect while preserving resources. Light-giving fibres include the peace silks (eri, muga, tussar [tussah], peduncle), contemporary cellulose tops (mint, soy, seaweed [SeaCell], rose), and the hackled linen. Other rare and specialist fibres to add into this section would be those of yak, angora (both goat and rabbit) and dog wool.

LOCKS AND CURLS

I am adding a special note on locks, that is clips of full curls that create a unique and authentic texture. Locks are densely packed fibres forming individual curls, and as such they add extra weight into the finished yarn if used in large quantities. Shearling locks are first-year lamb locks and are usually very small and soft, while other lock-clips can produce locks between 8cm-15cm (3⅛in–6in) long depending on the breed. Handling locks during carding can be done in a couple of ways depending on your needs:

METHOD ONE If the locks are clipped and individually separated, gently fan out the clipped edge, either by hand or with a small carding brush, and set them aside to add in *during spinning*. This will give you control over their inclusion, and allow you to add them in sections, to create unique blocks of texture as you go. You will be catching-in the fanned edge and letting the rest of the lock wrap around the yarn as you are spinning it; this forms a tight connection and looks really lovely.

METHOD TWO Adding locks into drum carding is something that requires a little experimentation, as with each turn of the drum, the lock curl will open up and lose definition. This provides a textural dimension within the batt and creates a more integrated batt ready for spinning. The way to add locks into a drum carder is best done by catching them onto the large drum as it goes around (see the photograph on page 47) rather than posting through the licker-in drum, as the lock can become stuck on the smaller drum and not roll onto the main batt smoothly. If there are areas of dense fibre, the drum carder will card them through although it may put pressure on the balance and timing of the drums, so finding ways to avoid unnecessary strain on your tools is important. Adding locks into the blending board in this way is easily done and retains much of the curl definition.

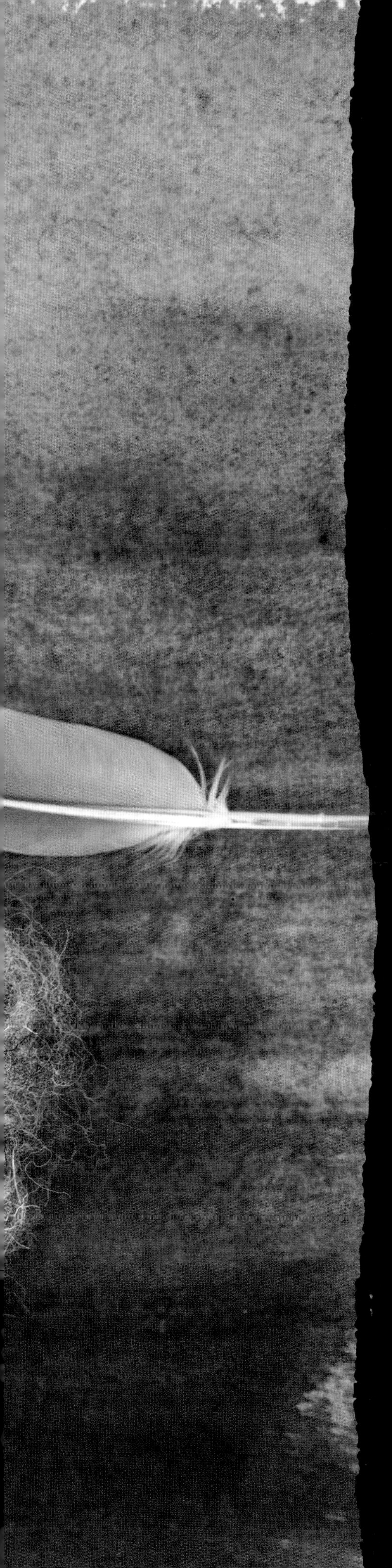

3

Spinning Beauty

This chapter explores hand spinning with hand spinners, supported spindles, drop spindles, kick spindles, spinning wheels and e-spinners (electric spinning wheels). Understanding the historical-cultural contexts of spindles and spinning wheels allows us to better grasp the most basic aspects of spinning as a craft-form in wholeness; the spinning of fibres into yarn.

'The spiral hook is drawn so that both dark and light, equally, form centers'

CHRISTOPHER ALEXANDER,
A Foreshadowing of 21st Century Art

DEFINITIONS

Spin (v) To revolve or gyrate; to whirl round.

Spinning (n) The action or operation of converting fibres into thread or yarn by hand-labour or by machinery.

The earliest known use of the noun spinning wheel is in the Middle English period (1150–1500); earliest evidence for the spinning wheel is from 1404.

Spindle (n) A simple instrument employed in spinning by hand, consisting of a slender rounded rod (usually of wood), tapering towards each end.

Oxford English Dictionary

Spindle (n) A round stick with tapered ends used to form and twist the yarn in hand spinning: the long slender pin by which the thread is twisted in a spinning wheel.

Merriam-Webster Dictionary

Hand Spinning Rhythm + Tension + Potential Energy = Spun Yarn

Types of Spindle

The spindle, in principle, is a simple stick of wood with a straight grain alignment and an even form that allows rotation, that in turn transfers the spin (or turning vortex of energy) into fibres to create yarn.

Early spindle types can be found in contemporary use, some in their original or historical form, and some with contemporary adaptations. Cultural and historical spinning tools were created to reflect the fibres in use, and the tool to best work with those fibres, at the time of origination. In cultures and lands that primarily work with cotton, which is traditionally finespun, we find spinning tools that support the spinning of cotton. The same principle applies to silk, which produces a fine and delicate yarn (or thread in its finest spin). Linen and flax fibres from the bast family also spin down into a very fine yarn, and so we can look at the spinning tools developed and used for these fibres as a study in mechanics, place and culture.

HAND SPINDLES

Hand spinners were held, grasped and turned. One of the earliest types is the Sami (Norse) *spinnekrok*, a forked branch turned in a circular motion by the wrist to create open-spun and wide-gauge (chunky) yarn, traditionally used in *Grene* weaving. The Mayan (South American) spinner employs the use of a swinging paddle around a stick, that is swung in rotation to increase the speed to spin string, rope and yarn – it's great fun to use. The Aboriginal-Australian spinning stick has a long slender axis stick pushed through a split-stick (or pair of sticks) to form a cross; it is worked by turning the stick in the hand to create a yarn or string of plant fibre or animal hide.

Coast Salish (Pacific North-west) and Cowichan Valley (British Columbia) indigenous spinning tools feature extremely large spindles and decorative whorls that are spun by turning the spindle with both hands while held aloft, the yarn being suspended from a ceiling hook and twisted in mid-air. Historically, these tools were used to spin local mountain goat wool combed with 'wool dog' hair, to create a Salish wool blend for cultural blankets. From the 1900s onwards, a contemporary blend of Salish wool using other locally sourced fibres to substitute for the earlier dog wool (as the 'wool dog' or Comox dog became extinct in the 1850s) was used to create traditional Cowichan knitwear (see Sewing-machine-adapted Spinner, page 70). The Coast Salish whorl motif is an important cultural totem that is often found in indigenous artwork, and is the central theme of large-scale carvings and art installations.

The Hutsul people of Ukraine use a handheld spindle and whorl, held down and away at arm's length, to spin the thick wool used for their traditional blankets and rugs. This spin produces an open bulky yarn that can be finished through a set of fulling processes; washing to tighten and shrink the yarns, drying the work then heavily brushing with hand carders after weaving to create a densely piled, soft surface.

DROP SPINDLES

Drop spindles use gravity to add tension and even distribution of the energy of the spin into the fibres. They can feature a tip with a carved notch or spiral, or the addition of a metal hook, to help to tension the spin. The gauge (or fineness/thickness) of your yarn is somewhat dictated by the maximum capacity of the notch or hook and therefore, in the case of hooked drop spindles, I recommend replacing the small hook with a larger hook (similar to a traditional cup-hook in a larger size) if possible, to allow

the potential to spin chunky-gauge or bulky yarn straight from the fleece.

Drop spindles are historically found in a wide range of cultures across North Africa, the Americas and Europe. They can be used for spinning most fibres that have a medium-to-long staple, and are suitable for spinning fine-gauge fibres, such as silk, cotton, linen and camelid, as well as mid-gauge fibres, such as goat and sheep's wool.

Generally, the design of the drop spindle employs a stick with a whorl (a wooden, clay or metal disk, or a pendulum or cross-stick), which provides additional weight to increase spin speed that increases tightness into the fibres for a firm yarn. A historical example from the Choctaw (Chahta) Nation shows a stick with a dried (unfired) clay whorl, identified as a drop spindle used to spin bison wool, and this forms part of a wonderful research paper into Choctaw (Chahta) craft tools by Jennifer Byram (see Bibliography). The Scottish *dealgan* is a weighted spinning tool constructed from a single block of wood that in effect acts as an integrated whorl, and is actioned in the same way as a whorled drop spindle.

The first experience with spinning for most beginners in contemporary crafts practices will be with a drop spindle that has a top whorl and a metal hook to tension the yarn. The pinch-and-park technique can assist in the early days, before using the gravitational feature of the drop spindle with confidence.

There is also the consideration of understanding one's dominant hand: spinning employs muscle memory, for correctly tensioning the spin, for pace and for how to work the hand(s) and spindle (or spinning wheel) into the correct rhythm and sequence. If one's dominant hand for writing is considered the starting place for the dominant hand in spinning, then you can experiment with ambidexterity and how that affects your final yarn and enjoyment of the craft. Rather than changing hands, I keep my spinning to the right hand, and when I use a supported spindle in the Navajo (Diné) way of spinning, that is all actioned on my right-hand side.

SUPPORTED SPINDLES

Supported spindles allow you to get into a relationship with the act of spinning without the (potential) stress and unpredictability of learning to spin on a drop spindle. Drop spindles, by their nature, have a weight limit to the amount of spun yarn you can wind onto the spindle before it becomes unbalanced or can no longer spin due to the weight of the yarn, and this necessitates more regular unloading of the spindle. When one is learning a craft, periods of repetition are necessary to develop muscle memory, and supported spindles can help you to get into the flow.

Supported spindles employ the assistance of a supporting element that makes direct contact with the lower tip of the spindle. This can simply be the floor itself, or a small wooden bowl placed on the floor (for longer spindles), or on a table or in the lap (for smaller spindles). I've used curved stones and hagstones as spinning supports in the past, when the need arose and I had to use whatever was to hand; however, stone is abrasive on spinning wood and I wouldn't recommend a stone or ceramic bowl for long-term use. It's best to spin wood on wood, or on the earth.

Tibetan spindles, small whorled spindles with a deep narrow whorl, are used with a spinning bowl. They were primarily developed to spin regional yak wool, a small-staple fibre that requires a tight spin to bring the fibres together into a yarn. Yak wool is also very dry, lacking the natural oils that inform the spin of sheep's wool for example, and spinning it requires some skill to emphasize the beautiful softness of this precious and challenging fibre.

Russian and French historical spindles that have integrated whorls within the body of the spindle itself (like the dealgan in principle, though with a slender form), skilfully moved between fingers and thumb, are held in the hand or used with a spinning bowl. It is possible to spin an adaptation in these styles by improvising with a chunky knitting needle, using the button-end as the whorl/weight.

GROUNDING – SPINNING IN RELATIONSHIP WITH THE FLOOR

The Navajo (Diné) spindle is an indigenous spinning tool originated by the south-west regional tribes of North America and New Mexico. Also called a south-west spindle, thigh spindle, lap spindle or floor spindle, it comprises a long spindle of around 75cm (29½in) with a whorled disk in the lower third to facilitate spin. The end of the spindle is either placed directly on the floor, or in a bowl on the floor, and is rested against the thigh on the side of the dominant hand (for me, that's my right side). The yarn is spun off the tip of the spindle, and the action of spin is 'rolled' along the thigh by using the fork between the thumb and index finger. This hand position is key to the technique as it adds strength, stability, control and balance to the spindle to allow a very fluid set of movements to become embodied. Rolling the spindle *back towards the body* creates a clockwise twist (Z twist yarn), and rolling the spindle *away from the body towards the knee* creates an anticlockwise spin (S twist yarn). (For more on twist direction, see Why Does Twist Direction Matter?, page 68) The Navajo (Diné) spindle is traditionally used to spin wool from the Navajo-Churro sheep breed (descended from the historic Spanish-Churra sheep) that has a double coat typical of more ancient sheep breeds, and that allows for the weaving of hardy rugs and saddle blankets.

Shorter-length spindles used in relationship to the ground include the supported spindle of the nomadic Berber (Amazigh) peoples of Northwest Africa with which they spin a blend of clipped camel and black goat hair used for making traditional tents. The spindle of around 50cm (20in), with a small whorl set near the lower tip, is used in a seated position on the ground, and rolled against the shin of an outstretched leg. In technique it is translatable to the Navajo (Diné) style of spinning, and offers insight into the oldest methods of tribal weaving and living heritages.

The choice to encounter cultural spinning should be done with full openness to research and reflection, acknowledging any sensitivities: cultural appreciation is to be encouraged; equally, cultural appropriation (the colonial approach of extracting cultural artefacts and methodologies) lacks respect and must be brought into correct balance. Thank you to all the indigenous, nomadic, tribal and minority ethnic craftspeople who have so generously allowed their works, tools, techniques and wisdom to be disseminated through craft networking and collaborative study in the age of technology. Without these teachers, it would be impossible to comprehend the depth and meaning of textile crafts as it pertains to our collective humanity and our shared spirituality.

To be clear: spinning yarn is considered as a gift from Above; replicating the great cosmic whorl and the rhythmic turning of the stars.

WHY DOES TWIST DIRECTION MATTER?

In principle, if you are spinning a single yarn, you can spin it whichever direction you wish. If you are intending to ply (combine strands) of yarn, then you must ply yarns together by reversing the original spin/twist direction. Therefore, if I spin my singles in a clockwise Z twist, I need to ply them all together in an anticlockwise S twist. This perhaps sounds more complex than it is in practice, so I invite you to experiment with the principles of direction of spin *and* direction of ply, and see what you learn about yourself in the process.

NAVAJO (DINÉ) CHAIN PLY

My preferred method of plying is to use the Navajo (Diné) chain-ply method, which forms a three-ply yarn, and here's the elegant part, *from a single spindle of spun yarn*. How does one create a three-stranded ply from only one thread? Let's explore more fully to appreciate this incredibly speedy way to create a perfectly balanced yarn.

In my experiments with different spindles and wheels, the Navajo (Diné) spindle produces the most consistent and balanced yarn, without overspin and without waste. I mention waste because spinning three bobbins on a wheel, and plying those three bobbins together often ends up with some 'waste' yarn for a variety of reasons: one or other of the bobbins runs fast; my hand tension might be out of balance; the spin might not be consistent between bobbins, etc. Chain ply, by its self-balancing method, creates *no* waste and *no* uneven balance to the ply, and because it is spun from an original single spindle's worth of yarn, the consistency in spin and overall look of the yarn is particularly pleasing.

Practically, the spinner needs only two spindles: one to create the original single yarn, and the second to ply back on to. As I mentioned earlier, the spinner simply reverses the direction of spin along the thigh, whist staying on the dominant side. The act of forming the chain, that is a loop with a length pulled through, is automatically measured by the spinner's arm's reach, and in the tensioning, the three strands are tensioned against each other, forming a beautifully balanced ply. If I spin on my wheel or e-spinner, I will often ply back using my Navajo (Diné) spindle because of the ease of the technique and the consistently well-balanced results that are comfortably achieved.

I consider Clara Sherman (1914-2010) to be my instructor in the Navajo (Diné) way of spinning, and I would like to pay my respects to her as a craft teacher and to the work she created as an artist of the Navajo (Diné) Nation. Clara made her spinning tutorial available to the world, and through her guidance and sharing I have gained a very precious craft skill for which I am incredibly grateful. Clara's work was part of the textile collection offered at the Toadlena Trading Post, New Mexico, home to the Two Grey Hills tradition of Navajo (Diné) weaving. The cultural weaving of this region continues through the work of many others. Lynda Teller Pete and Barbara Teller Ornelas, daughters of Navajo (Diné) weaver Ruth Teller, are authors of the wonderful book *How to Weave a Navajo Rug and Other Lessons from Spider Woman*. TahNibaa Naataanii is a spinner and weaver who shares her traditional teaching practice of preparing and spinning Navajo-Churro wool for use in her weaving arts practice. Ephraim Anderson, known professionally as Zefren-M, is a contemporary Navajo (Diné) weaver who is reviving Navajo-Churro sheep stocks for cultural spinning and weaving with Rainbow Fiber Co-Op.

Other important historical cultural spinning styles include Haida (Pacific Northwest Coast) and Tlingit (Alaskan) thigh-spun warp that is core-spun with soaked cedar bark (to naturally prevent moths), as used for traditional ceremonial regalia weavings for Chilkat and Raven's Tail designs, as practised by contemporary indigenous weavers Lily Hope (Tlingit) and Evelyn Vanderhoop (Haida).

KICK SPINDLE

Kick spindles are a contemporary adaptation in spinning that bring together elements from different spindle types to create a unique tool. Placed on the floor, this spindle is mounted on a base and has a large, heavy whorl that is kicked to perpetuate spin, which is then extended by the use of bearings, allowing a fast and rapid set of rotations per kick. The spindle aspect is based on the point of a great wheel design (see Spinning Wheels), and the yarn can be spun fine or midweight, with a relatively long draw from the tip of the spindle to the full extension of the arm. The kick spindle I use is a handmade design in cherry and maple woods made by Jim Echter of True Creations Woodturning in the USA, and it is a particularly portable design that flat packs into its base board (see image on page 62).

SEWING-MACHINE-ADAPTED SPINNERS

There are some wonderful examples of the traditional treadled Singer-style flatbed sewing machines of the Victorian and Edwardian era having been converted into spinners. I've found references to historic examples in the indigenous Coast Salish craft communities in the Cowichan Valley knitting tradition of the 1900s, as well as the spinner used by contemporary London weaver Rachel Scott Bowling.

More recently, Anthony Harrison-Griffin has designed i-SPIN, a 3D-printed unit that can be installed on to a domestic sewing machine to conveniently turn it into an e-spinner.

SPINNING WHEELS

The spinning wheel is an icon of archetypal craft folklore: maidens spinning flax, enchanted spindles – the stuff of dreams! That being said, for the many historic versions of the spinning wheel, we have an equal number of contemporary adaptations, as we will explore.

Early spinning wheels from India and China utilized a hand-crank to turn the wheel, and featured a fine-pointed spindle for cotton and silk spinning. Reference images of the time show craftspeople seated on the floor or on low benches at the hand-turned spinning wheels.

Representations of the well-known *great wheel*, or 'walking wheel', the hand-turned spinning wheel popular in Europe, feature in medieval manuscripts such as the Luttrell Psalter. It's commonly understood that the fateful 'spindle' of the Sleeping Beauty fairy tale took the form of a great wheel, and because of the Grimm Brothers' research locations in Bavaria, could have been for spinning either wool or linen (in the case of linen, a distaff would have been used too).

ANATOMY OF THE SPINNING WHEEL

The Mother-of-All holds
the tension and
The twin maidens;
The maidens hold the spindle
Or, they hold the flyer,
which holds the bobbin,
which winds the spun yarn;
The spinner walks the wheel
Or treadles the footman,
Who turns the wheel, in turn

Spinning Timeline

SPINDLES In the prehistoric and ancient cultural worlds, simple wooden spinning sticks would have been used after the development of hand-twining and ropemaking. Some of the very earliest spindle designs are represented by the spinning sticks with a split axis used by Aboriginal-Australians and the Choctaw (Chahta) wooden spindle with applied mud whorl (see Hand Spindles on page 60).

SPINDLES WITH WHORLS Palaeolithic and Neolithic (the Old and New Stone Ages), archaeological evidence of whorls.

CHINESE SPINNING WHEEL c. 400-200 BCE, silk wheel.

CHARKA WHEEL (OR BOOK CHARKA) Indian antiquity to present day, cotton wheel.

GREAT (OR WALKING) WHEEL c. medieval period, European, wool and linen. In Scotland, this type of wheel was called a *muckle*.

SAXONY (OR SAXON) WHEEL c. 1600s Germany. Angled wheel with a one-sided treadle, where the elements of wheel and flyer are positioned in a (sometimes sloping) landscape alignment, traditionally for spinning linen. The Ashford Traditional spinning wheel is a contemporary (since the 1970s) adaptation of the Saxony wheel.

NORWEGIAN WHEEL c. 1800s, this has a definite horizontal line to the structure with a wooden shelf or ledge and is typical of spinning wheels used in Scandinavia.

CASTLE (OR UPRIGHT) WHEEL c. 1800s Scotland and Ireland. A vertically stacked wheel with the flyer positioned directly below or above the wheel. The Ashford Country Spinner is a double-treadle adaptation of a castle wheel built into a fixed frame.

DOUBLE-TREADLE A relatively contemporary adaptation in the history of spinning wheels, this style allows front-on ergonomic balance for moving the spinning wheel by alternating left and right-foot pressure. I researched evidence of adapted or improvised vintage wheels with double-treadles: one in particular was an Arts and Crafts era (c.1880–1920) adaptation from a wooden chair, attributed to G. Gower, featuring a double-treadle.

KICK-SPINDLE This type of spindle is fairly rare and a real talking point when shared with fellow spinners. It features three elements: a base, a spindle-stick and a large whorl to be kicked with the foot. The addition of metal ball-bearings within the whorl and/or base, allows the rotations to continue for some time with just a single kick.

E-SPINNER An electronic spinner combining a bobbin and maiden with a motor and foot pedal as a wheel-and-treadle substitute, similar to a domestic sewing machine pedal. If placed on a high desk or kitchen worktop, they can be used standing, and I've heard of spinners using them in campervans and even on boats, due to their portability, size, stability and ease of use.

KRAFFT SW1 A contemporary spinning wheel prototype by designer Oliver Sunderland, the KRAFFT SW1 was shortlisted for the 2018 Cræftiga Prize by Hole & Corner, and is manufactured in metals and wood. Oliver's vision connects the practical tool of the spinning wheel with the form of the spinning wheel as a domestic object, constituting a piece of furniture it its own right.

How to Spin

I like to be extremely practical with my tuition, so the following insights are invitations to experiment and explore aspects such as the following: what type of spin you might like to attempt; what comes naturally; how you feel about the results you get; how challenging you find the act of spinning; how enjoyable you find it; what your yarn is showing you about your tension, rhythm, flexibility and attitude.

Firstly, let me be incredibly direct: spinning yarn can be as simple or as complicated as you need it to be for yourself. So, here are some questions to consider before you approach your chosen tools:

- Do you have a pre-determined idea of how yarn should or shouldn't be?
- Do you believe there is a correct or incorrect way of spinning yarn?
- Are you attached to 'perfect' outcomes?
- Can you tolerate the unpredictable?
- Are you able to remain teachable by the materials and tools themselves?
- Are you in tune with your body and your breathing?

These questions may seem equally unimportant *and* challenging. However, what is important is that you're undoing any introjected ideas about right/wrong, should/must, perfect/messy, and other extreme dichotomies of perfectionism and correctness. Let's be flexible and practical. We are spinning yarn, one of the most ancient and instinctive of human gestures. There doesn't *need* to be a planned or designed outcome, with weights, measures, lengths, counting, sketching, planning; there is no *need* for the yarn to be anything other than a reflection of the materials and processes that bought it into wholeness; *let the yarn guide outcomes.* I make this point because jumping into design planning can be a creative block because it places the focus on a predicted outcome and has the potential to bypass the creative act of craft itself. By removing the weight of expectation, we can genuinely allow our craft to reveal the next steps – but first, let us spin.

KNOWING YOUR STUFF

Varieties of fibre preparations that you may encounter:

RAW Animal fibres are clipped, sheared, combed or pulled (by natural shedding) straight from the sheep, goat, alpaca, camel, rabbit, dog, yak and other fibre-giving creatures. This usually arrives in sacks, and with sheep's wool, a shear-for-spinning fleece will have been rolled up in such a way that it can be unrolled by the spinner to assess the areas to be used. Raw wool might be in any state of cleanliness, from totally raw to skirted, picked, tumbled, soaked, or scoured (see Chapter Two, pages 49–50, for more on this).

ROVING (SLIVER, PENCIL, BUMP) This is a length of fibre that has been fully scoured clean and carded into continuous lengths, and coiled into sacks. *Sliver roving* is quite substantial, and you may want to strip it into four smaller slivers before spinning, or pull it into softer tufts for blending. *Pencil roving* is incredibly thin roving ready to spin fine yarn, and you can create your own pencil roving by stripping down slivers. A *bump* is a prepared large roll or ball of roving, and it can be used for spinning directly, or for pulling out sections for blending.

SILK Wild silk (also called peace silk) is the collection of discarded and hatched silk cocoons from specific craft traditions found in India. These are naturally shaded, undyed fibres with a range of texture, and they are provided in roving and waste-silk cakes. The more widely used silk production method of very finely spun silks is achieved by propagating mulberry-silk cocoons that are picked before hatching. These are boiled to unglue the cocoons to produce the incredibly long filament fibres, which are then spooled in continuous lengths. The price for this unbroken thread is an unhatched, dead silk moth, raising the question of craft ethics. Spider silk has also attracted ethical controversy in recent years, due to harvesting methods on live spiders and the parallel developments of genetic modifications of spider-silk proteins with other animals, including silkworms and associated silk-production methods.

CLOUD Fibre that has been pinched, pulled and blended roughly by hand.

COMBED Wool taken from English wool combs (use water and oil spray to reduce static).

HACKLED Whether hackled by hand or comb, fibre can be stacked and built up on the face of the hackle and removed by using a diz.

DIZ This tool is used to pull a sliver of fibre off a full hackle of combed fibre, and variously sized holes on the diz allow you to choose the thickness or fineness of the pulled sliver (see page 33).

HAND-CARDED ROLAGS These are smaller rolags ready to spin from the end.

DRUM-CARDED BATTS These large batts can be rolled and spun from the end, as you would a smaller rolag (see the image on page 34); alternatively, the flat batt can be spun from a corner or fold, or it can be stripped into smaller slivers.

SPINNING FROM THE FOLD This technique involves folding a flat batt of fibre like a book, then using the apex of the fold to draw out the fibre. Smaller batts can be folded around the index fingertip, then drawn off the tip of the finger where the fold is sitting.

HOW TO BLEND AS YOU SPIN

Pieced-blending is a simple and effective method to create a batch yarn that is essentially spun in segments, featuring different yarns (by texture or shade), and each segment added grows the yarn. It's a great way of sampling a variety of fibres in one bobbin or spindle and of practising your joining technique. Fibres can be selected in lengths of your choosing (roving), and you can experiment with roving lengths of different shades, tones and textures, exploring graduated ombré and/or contrasting humbug.

NOTES ON TERMINOLOGY

Ombré An optic technique of graduating shading from light to dark (or vice versa) in a subtle and pleasing colour shift. A good example of ombré in textiles is seen in Shibori, the Japanese technique of indigo dye work, which among its many resist techniques includes dip-dyeing to create this effect. (My own exploration of indigo-vat Shibori ombré was facilitated at Dyehaus in the Blue Mountains of Australia, and the ways of working both dry and wet cloth by dipping and grading the indigo from palest blue to richest ink.)

Humbug This term, perhaps best associated with traditional black-and-white-striped boiled sweets, has its roots in the language of the ancient Nordic mythology of shadows and ghosts, which is an elegant expression of this light-dark contrast.

Spinning: Two Ways to 'Wild Yarn'

My Main Spinning Tools

These are the Navajo (Diné) spindle and the Ashford e-spinner Super Jumbo/Ashford Country Spinner: the electric e-spinner and the manual spinning wheel models use the same 1kg (35oz) bobbin interchangeably, depending on my needs. I use these tools independently, and also in combination when plying.

SELECTING YOUR FIBRE

If you are a beginner spinner, the best advice I've heard and which I'll add to is as follows: buy 1kg (35oz) of fibre. It should have some texture to provide grip, and this will be a *core-spun* yarn to help you get acquainted with the pull/draw of the fibre without too much frustration of breaking threads. Herdwick wool is particularly textured and full of kemp, and I find it a very helpful yarn for beginning and practising. It may be tempting to start with a soft fibre, such as Bluefaced Leicester, Merino, or shorter staple soft Shetland; however, these very soft fibres will slip and pull out of your hand until you get to grips with the speed and timing of a spinning wheel or e-spinner, or the gravity of a drop spindle. The Navajo (Diné) spindle is by far the most supportive tool, and perhaps allows a more integrated experience of learning to spin, before attempting more mechanical wheels and spinners that have their own particular demands.

THE IMPORTANCE OF WATER

Keeping a small cup of water nearby as you spin will come in very useful, particularly for spinning linen and bast fibres, which need moisturizing as you spin and join.

KEEP SPINNING

By the time you have spun up that first kilo, you will have become familiar with the ways of your hands and tools, the movements and the timings. Your finished yarn might be full of back-twist and knots from stressful re-joins, and the core spinning thread might be on the outside instead of on the inside. You might have lost your temper more than once and invoked plenty of colourful expletives, and perhaps even wept, just as every other apprentice spinner before you. But look, you have spun your first kilo, and that counts for something. Well done!

The best way to become a competent craftsperson is to practise in the early days for as long as possible in one sitting. Therefore, after the successful completion of the first kilo, repeat the process with a second kilo, this time working with the fibre alone (or starting with a core-spin until you feel able to cut the cord, so to speak). I advise using the same fibre as before, for consistency and continuity.

Spinning Techniques for Energetic Mark Making

EXERCISE – EXPLORE YOUR FIBRE

Take a handful of fibre, encounter it, establish contact: touch, texture, weight, softness, scent. Pull and stretch the fibres, find the spaces of strength and fragmentation, seek the limits and the particles. How delicate a single filament is, how strong a bundle...

TWIST A twist is a spiral, and yarn is a spiral formed in three-dimensions (and fixed by balancing with water and gravity). We can think about spirals in nature: Fibonacci, tornado, whirlpool, vortex, sycamore seed flight...

PINCH The pinch of your fingers acts as a dam to control and halt the flow of the spin. The spin travels along the fibre like a wave and hits your fingertips at the pinch. Once you feel and observe that the yarn is the correct consistency for your needs, hold the pinch and, with the other hand, draw out more fibre, then release the pinch and watch the energy flow into the fibre, creating the spiral of yarn.

DRAFT Drafting is the lengthening-out of fibres to the anticipated thickness or fineness required to achieve the spin you need. Roving or batts can be pre-drafted and set aside in a basket ready for spinning proper; or you can draft as you spin in one smooth rhythmic motion, in either short or long-draw techniques.

DRAW The draw is the active drafting during spinning, and the draw can be short or long depending on your technique. *Long draw* involves fully extending your arm while holding tension in the fibres, allowing the energy of the spin to travel all the way up to your fingertips, known as the pinch. Long draw is possible on the kick spindle and the Navajo (Diné) spindle, as well as spinning wheels, and the result is usually a very well-balanced mid-to-fine yarn gauge. *Short draw* is when twist is fed in to the yarn in smaller sections to allow greater control, and is a good technique for spinning incredibly chunky yarn, very wild yarn with lots of texture, or for more detailed needs such as adding in locks or core spinning. For beginners, short draw on a drop spindle using the pinch-and-park technique gives you good control of the process: pinch the fibre a little way away from the hook, add spin by turning the spindle in your hand, park the spindle between the knees, then slide the pinch farther along the roving, allowing the energy of the spin to travel up to your fingertips, creating yarn.

FEED OF YARN ONTO A SPINNING WHEEL
On a wheel, 'feed' is the speed of uptake onto the bobbin, and the feed of the yarn is dictated by the tension on the bobbin and how fast it is flying. One has to learn the choreography of the spinning wheel to dance with this rhythm, the draw and the feed, to and fro. On a manual spinning wheel or an e-spinner, the bobbin will have capacity for adjustable tension, and also the wheel's drive band might have variable settings; between these two functions, you can get a nicely balanced spin and feed that is smooth and gentle and doesn't grab or pull, or split the roving, or overspin your yarn. This takes some time and patience to figure out, so best be in a mindful, calm place when first encountering spinning wheels and e-spinners.

FEED OF YARN ONTO A SPINDLE This is manual, so there's a stop after a length of yarn has been spun, and keeping the yarn under tension, the yarn is wound onto the spindle to form a cop near to the whorl. This adds to the whorl's weight and should be done in a way that provides even balance to the whole spindle.

JOINING Roving and batts need to be joined in as you spin and use up the fibre in your hand. Joining is really simple and can be helped by keeping a small cup of water to hand to dampen the fibres at the join.

JOINING-IN METHOD When you are approaching the end of your fibre section, stop spinning and place the final 5cm (2in) on your thigh, then open this section equally to form a shallow V shape. Taking the fresh end of your new fibre roving or batt, place it into the gap you have created. Splash on a little water, then begin spinning again, keeping a firm pinch on the section, allowing it to slightly overspin. Release all the spin into this section, and watch the join disappear into your new section of yarn. Using this joining-in method, you can change fibres as often as desired to create a variegated, blended yarn as you spin (see How to Blend as You Spin on page 78).

CORE SPIN This is a simple way to create yarn by wrapping your main fibre around a finer yarn or thread. The core can be any thread you have on a cone, placed on the floor for ease of spooling. I have successfully used linen, wool and nettle blends as well as cotton-linen blends to core spin; however, thin-gauge wool used as a core thread has the tendency to snap under too much pull or tension, from a spinning wheel for example, which is not helpful in this instance.

PLY Plying yarn involves twisting or combining multiple strands, and this can be a really fun and revelatory part of yarn development, as different sections combine to form new, sometimes surprising textures and conversations.

EXERCISE
TWIST AND THROW

A simple and spontaneous exercise is to take a length of spun yarn and, with the help of a friend, a hook or a chair, create a long loop with two strands, holding it under tension. Then release the counter-balance (friend, hook or chair) and throw the yarn into the air. Retrieve it to see how your yarn has naturally plied, enfolded and twisted around itself like serpents of DNA.

4

Yarn Finishing

It is important to develop a set of finishing techniques for your yarn, so that when it comes time to use it in a project, you can be sure of its behaviour based on preparation.

For my work, primarily in weaving, I have the following technical needs so that I can weave with confidence: wet-finishing and hanging with weights. This ensures that the blended hank of yarn is brought together in warm water and that any potential energy from the spin is dispersed and evenly distributed throughout the hank. It also provides a soaking wash to clean the yarn, and then, by using the combination of water, gravity and ceramic weights, pulls out any overspin and fully balances the yarn by stretching out any bounce*; the water being pulled by the additional weight and the force of gravity, helping to facilitate a dependable yarn. (*Knitters may want to retain bounce, so please experiment with lighter weights or no weights in the hang.)

In whatever way you develop your best finishing practice, using the same technique with each yarn batch is especially important when using wild-yarn blends. While your fibre content may differ considerably between hanks, the finishing technique ensures balance and consistency across a variegated batch. This is an aspect of craft discipline that will allow you to be confident with your outcomes as you progress, applying the simple equation 'methodology + repetition', or a more time-honoured expression would be 'practice makes perfect'.

SETTING THE TWIST

It is traditional to rest the spun yarn to allow it to settle into its new, twisted form, dispelling the potential energy of the spin to bounce back through the yarn and essentially untwist sections or create uncontrollable loops. You can set the twist by simply leaving the yarn on the spindle or bobbin for a day, a few days, or longer.

An additional step to resting and preparing the yarn is to use a wonderfully named tool, the *niddy-noddy*, to wind a hank of yarn off the bobbin. This is done by applying tension and tightly winding the yarn around the ends of the cross-sticks, effectively balancing the twist while measuring meterage. Each loop of the niddy-noddy equates to a certain length (1.5m, for example). Therefore, by counting the finished loops, one can calculate exact meterage. The hobby-horse-like movement of the niddy-noddy in action lends itself to its delightfully onomatopoeic name. A beautiful example of this tool can be seen in a painting attributed to Leonardo da Vinci, *Madonna of the Yarnwinder*, c. 1500.

Yarn can also be left on the niddy-noddy (if your tool is not in demand) for a further rest; otherwise, it is removed and twisted under tension into a hank, sometimes called a skein. Technically, a skein is a style of yarn finishing which includes a standard unit of measure, traditionally used by weaving mills to account for yardage in batch consistency for planning large bolts of cloth, for example. A measured and wound hank is a skein, and your niddy-noddy is also a measuring device. Each loop-around the tool is equal to a standard measurement, and multiplied by the number of strands in a loop so you can work out your overall meterage. This is the subtle and helpful distinction between hank and skein.

It is usual to tie off the ends of the yarn around the full width of the loops to secure them, and to add a few lightly knotted scrap loops of yarn (linen or cotton works well and can be reused if not tied too tightly) to ensure the hank stays aligned during the next step, which is the soaking stage.

SOAKING THE HANK

Prepare a bowl or basin with warm water and a little wool wash or a non-foaming shampoo. It is best to use a ceramic or enamelled bowl, as metal containers can change the colour of botanically dyed yarns; for example, a tannin-pink can turn a mauve-purple in a metal vessel (the same principle applies to metallic washing machine drums). Introduce the hank in its twisted state and allow the water to be absorbed. After around 30 minutes, untwist the hank and let the yarn find its balance by spreading out in the water, leaving it to soak for an hour or so, or overnight if you have the time and space.

A NOTE ON OTHER WINDING TOOLS

The swift, or umbrella swift, (in Norway, I was told my antique swift was called 'the grumpy old woman') is used to wind-off a finished, dried hank of yarn ready for crafting, either by winding into a ball, or winding directly onto a shuttle for weaving.

The spinner's weasel is a larger tool that is more like a wrap reel or warping mill, which spins and measures meterage of yarn to historically understood tariffs for standardized textiles, and used during the medieval guild era and throughout the industrialized era of textiles, c. 1400s-1800s.

Contemporary artist Will Cruikshank makes his own experimental spindles, winding and spinning machines to create large artworks exploring the processes of winding yarn. His machines include adaptations of potters wheels, lathes and cement mixers.

Making a Moth-resistant Leave-in Soak, Dip or Spray

Horse chestnut soap has been referenced by textile historian Sally Pointer as being a moth-resistant addition to early 1800s cloth production (*New Family Recipe Book*, 1824). Cedarwood and cedar oil renders fibres unable to hold moths' eggs and so is universally known as a protective medium for woollen items. The best way to create a protective wool-spray or soak is as follows:

- 50ml (1.7 US fl oz) amber glass bottle with spray head – amber glass prevents condensation and evaporation via sunlight
- Distilled water – this is free from mineral and salt residues
- Witch-hazel-extract solution – a natural emulsifier (and conditioning cleanser) that helps to disperse and suspend very fine particles of essential oils into a sprayable liquid
- *Horse-chestnut extract – prepared in a vegetable glycerine base rather than an alcohol-based tincture, or make your own using (heated) distilled water and a muslin (cheesecloth) to strain out the grated horse-chestnut pieces
- Glycerine – beneficial for fibre conditioning, this should be added minimally at a ratio of 10:1, i.e. ten parts water to one part glycerine
- **Essential oils, cedar and lavender – for their moth-resistant properties and traditional textile scents

METHOD

Half-fill the amber bottle with approx. 25ml (0.85 US fl oz) of witch-hazel solution, then add 5 drops of horse chestnut in glycerine extract (or just glycerine on its own).

Add around 15-20 drops total of essential oils in a mix you like: cedar is very strongly scented, so you might want to add 10 drops lavender and 5 drops cedar, for example, or any mix ratio of your preference up to a maximum of 20 drops.

Top up to the bottleneck with either plain distilled water, or more witch-hazel extract, or horse chestnut in distilled water extract (if you have made some).

Affix the spray head to the bottle and shake the mixture until the oil particles are finely diffused in the solution. Test the spray to see if the scent works for your needs.

USE

For a protective and refreshing spritzer onto fleece, yarn and finished items: lightly spray and leave to air dry.

Alternatively, the spray mix can be used as the base for a final soaking or rinsing solution, designed to be left in to penetrate and coat the fibres, to get the best from the herbal properties.

Safety notes:
*The horse chestnut can transfer a pink-brown tint, so I don't recommend its use on white-based blends, in case there is any unintended dyeing.
** Pregnant women should avoid direct contact with essential oils due to contraindications.

Finishing the Yarn

Remove the saturated yarn from the soak water, using stainless steel or copper kitchen hooks (again, beware of metallic changes to botanical dyes – however at this stage the contact surface area is minimal). Hang the yarn somewhere suitable to drip-dry, but do not use iron hooks as these will rust. The water in combination with gravity will assist the balancing of the spin and dispel any final energy. For knitters, this may be enough to provide you with a balanced yarn that still maintains its natural elastic bounce. However, for weavers, I'd advise adding a heavy ceramic weight (or a mug filled with water) hooked to the lowest point of the hank, to pull out any elasticity, for a more predictable weave with minimal shrinkage on the width.

When using yarns from different batches, it is important that all the finishing is done in the same way. This will prevent an unhappy wobbly selvedge due to unbalanced shrinkage between a weighted yarn and an unweighted yarn that retained its bounce; this bounce will effectively 'pull in' that section of weaving and create a dent in the edge of your woven cloth after the final work is soaked, and this may not be obvious during weaving.

It is possible to source reproduction fired-clay loom weights for warp-weighted looms, and I have a beautiful handmade glazed set gifted by Lily Aisbitt-Waugh. I also have an unglazed set of ten weights from a historical reproduction maker, Living Past UK, based on the Coppergate dig finds in York, weighing 350g (12½oz) each. A good yarn weight kit would be: ten fired-clay weights and 20 large kitchen S-hooks (in stainless steel or copper).

Once weighted and dried, twist your hank for storage, or wind into a ball with the help of a swift or other winder tool.

A NOTE ON GRAVITY

My pattern-cutting hero is Madeleine Vionnet (1876-1975), whose innovative set of methods and techniques were the subject of my BA final project and dissertation in 2004. Her achievements and outcomes were so sublimely excellent that I cannot omit her impact on my creative life here in my book about yarn. How can a French fashion designer from the 1930s be influential on a yarn spinner in 2024? The answer is, by her use and understanding of gravity and weights.

In order to achieve the fluid bias drape that was her signature cut, Vionnet needed to embody the wisdom of physics: how fabric contains a hidden dimension (the bias grain), and how to manipulate and manage this invisible dimension, by understanding the plane-angles of the body (the breasts, hips, the swing of the spine), and placing a gravitational intervention between the primary pattern cutting and the final, definitive cut. Vionnet would hang her pre-cut panels in the correct alignment corresponding to the solid plane of the body it would be flowing off (a dimensional anchor point, such as a hip bone, for example), and then she would suspend weights from the hem of the panel, using either small leaded cloth weights or clips (closely spaced clothes pegs work very well). These would be left in place for at least a week, with regular steaming to encourage this invisible bias element to be pulled down and out of the cloth by the force of gravity, thereby shaping it into a balanced and controlled piece of cloth ready for final cutting and sewing.

The elegance of Vionnet's technique is something I will never forget, and so to bring even a moment of it into yarn spinning is my tribute to her.

5

Curating & Collecting

Curating yarn is the realm of the dedicated craftsperson who deeply appreciates yarn as its own expressive medium; and the stash, as it's known, is the considered selection and collection of said yarns. This collection might contain your own handspun yarns, purchased yarns, commissioned yarns or yarns made to other spinners' visions, vintage finds, or more commercially produced yarn. My own collection has moved through all of these iterations in combination.

Curating & Collecting as a Design Process

Curating your yarn stash marks the beginning of the design process, or if you want to be fully trusting of the intuitive-creative process, it can be the entirety of the design process. Let me elaborate...

When we think of 'design', and often when we train formally in textile design, there is a space in between the materials and the action of craft, that being the realm of the sketchbook. Sometimes the sketchbook is a primary object and the material considerations are connected with the design after the fact, as a retrofitted aspect. Sometimes the white pages of a new sketchbook present a physical creative barrier and psychological block to action. As an experimental pattern cutter, I was a materials-lead practitioner, and I would let the material show me what form it wished to take across the entire process; in the garment shape, construction and finishing. There was a symbiosis between materiality and the flat-lay of the pattern, with a sketchbook becoming more of a diary and recipe book of notes as I gained confidence in my process. Since I turned my attention to yarn work and weaving, I have let go of sketchbooks and go straight to my materials. My approach to design is much more based on trust; trusting the materials and the yarns, and moving them between my hands from a raw form, then a yarn form, into a woven form.

In this way, and to use some art therapy language, *I get out of my own way*; or to speak somatically, *I get out of my head and into my hands*. I don't have a pre-determined idea of an outcome, I don't follow a sketch or pattern. Instead, I literally go with the flow and see what happens. I think in the world of craft this creative self-trust needs more amplification.

A simple way of transitioning from yarns to loom (for example), is to lay out or hang up your hanks in the sequence in which you desire to weave them. This arranging or organizing of order can be the design process in completion: a series of choices, based on instinct, whereby we have already chosen the yarn for its inherent qualities and our own responses to its textural nature. In this way the organic arrangement flows into the final work, which is somewhat of a surprise once it is unrolled and seen in its wholeness. I then hang up the finished work, regard it and sit with it, and respond to the overall feeling of encountering the work. I acknowledge I am in a creative relationship with my work, and we are having a conversation.

The next work I make builds upon this experience and encounter, and growing a body of work in this way connects mindfulness, meaning and craft into a creative cycle of self-expression and self-reflection. To go a step further, placing the works back into the landscape to review them adds another layer of conversation and relationship between your craft and your environment. In this way, craft practice becomes expansive, connective, holistic and therapeutic.

This is why curating and collecting your stash from a place of joy, interest and freedom is the root and key to a finished work that feels like you accurately interpreted the essence of the raw material; that it represents some of the wildness you felt and the emotional qualities and stories of the materials themselves. When considering these points, in recognition of the creative potential in any particular yarn to convey these aspects into and within a finished work, we start to see how a materials-lead practice deepens the personal experience of craft and forms a space of narrative textiles with the capacity to tell the stories of our time.

Reasons for Growing a Yarn Collection

These are many, however some familiar needs yarn collectors will recognize include:

- Small batch yarn which is non-repeatable
- Finding a stunning yarn that simply must go in the collection
- Curating yarns on a theme, by shade or fibre, for example
- Collecting yarns towards a specific project
- Yarns to study as primary research
- Yarns to swatch and sample with
- Yarns to inspire
- For the love of looking at a well-crafted stash and feeling pure joy
- To participate in international craft exchanges, such as FibreShare (which I hope returns soon)

GENTLE TASK

Think about the paths to inspiration that you have walked as you've been reading: the lands, landscapes, seasons, elements, textures, shades, themes and feelings that you have been contemplating, noting and experiencing. Take time to vision three elements:

wool, shell, winter

or

fire, smoke, autumn

or

spider, pewter, rain

The Selkie (2018)

With this, my first woven collection and exhibition, I used a selection of elemental touchstones, in a similar spirit to the examples given in the gentle task above, and I reimagined these into the folk story of the same name. The Selkie myth gave me a deep dive into archetypal symbolism, textures, shades, and deep emotional process, while simultaneously connecting me to the islands of Orkney and to Teresa Probert's heritage flock (see Chapter One).

This gives you a way into a deeper connection with your yarn curation: the yarn means something to you, and connecting with what that is holds much potential for your journey forward into craft. Your experience of your world and the stories within it provide an endless wellspring of inspiration.

Research your key words, get a clear sense of shade and texture direction, and begin sourcing and collecting elements that will support your yarn creation: paint a picture.

Whether you purchase, commission or spin your own yarn at the very start of your curating process, take time to encounter these yarns with your full spectrum of senses – optics, scent, touch, emotion – allowing the yarn to reflect back your own state of mind and being.

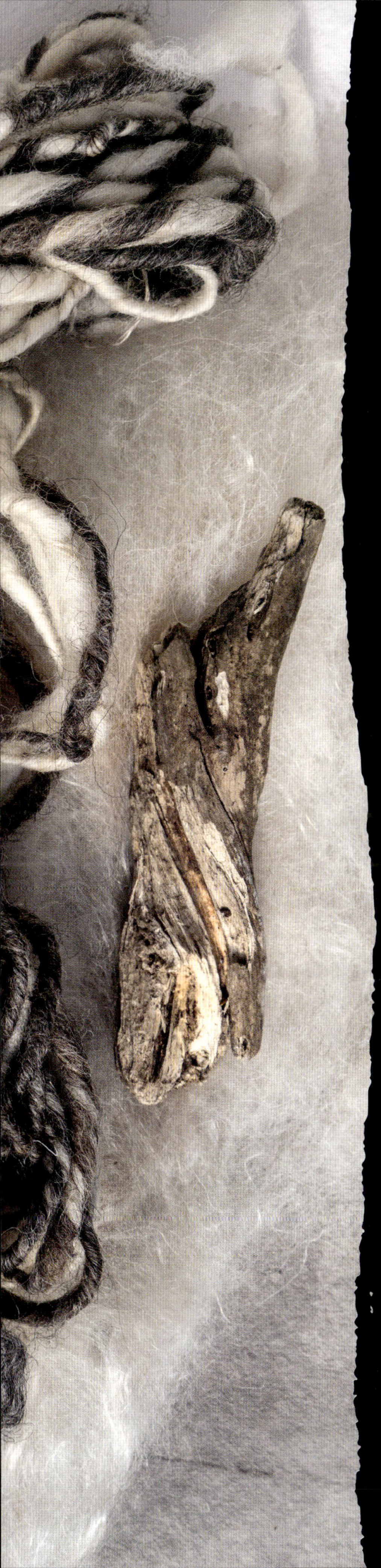

6

Projects Ideas

Handspun yarn provides opportunities to encounter the unpredictable and the variegated in our crafts practices. There may be many questions around how to manage areas of thickness, shrinkage, tension, etc.… the best teacher is indeed the yarn itself, and here are some reflections on what my yarn has taught me so far.

VARIEGATION Handspun yarn can be so free that one skein contains an area as thick as unspun carded roving, and a few metres later, it becomes as thin as a spider's web. That being the case, how can one possibly work with such dramatic variegation? The good news is, quite well! This comes back to your signature spin: the rhythm of your spin – where bulk appears and where fine thread appears – is actually more organized than you may at first assume. Once you start crafting with the yarn, whether in knit, crochet, weave, etc., you start to see the signature manifest in the work, and begin to appreciate the implicit quality of textile to accommodate this variety. The whole moves to meet the areas of fullness and sparsity by balancing these aspects across the whole work, but it takes trust to work in an unpredictable way to see the bigger pattern unfolding. In this regard, working with handspun yarn is really quite magical; it is also philosophical and meditative, and creates works of astounding personal meaning and reflective depth.

'before the process of weaving, there is the process of yarn preparation, and before this the raw materials must be selected… Yarn itself can be a thing of beauty, even before it is woven…'

THEO MOORMAN,
Weaving as an Art Form

TENSION A relaxed tension is needed to allow for the denser aspects to be gently included in the crafted work. In this way, the element of *space* needs to be welcomed so the work can breathe and feel airy. Bringing personal tension into a work will translate into the finished piece, so I encourage you to check in with your breathing, your hands and your posture when working with your handspun yarns.

THE WEB Fully submerging and soaking the finished work will allow any movement, accommodation, balancing and redistribution of tension and potential energy remaining in the spin to dissipate. Flat-lay blocking is essential to assist the final work forming into its finished structure. The aspect of water (or indeed steam) in the finishing processes is really necessary for handspun yarns to relax and settle.

SHRINKAGE The final soak should be at a hand-warm temperature to ensure any future cold soaks won't encourage further shrinkage. As a maker, it is important to be in control of the unpredictable nature of wet-finishing at this stage, as you won't be able to assist once the work has left your studio. In this regard, you want to preshrink without too much drama, and advise future *cold soaking only* to your clients. With my handspun yarn used for my weaving, I can safely estimate 5cm-10cm (2in–4in) shrinkage on the width and 15cm-20cm (6in–8in) on the length of finished works after wet-finishing. This is a combination of the yarn tightening up, as well as the warp taking-up the empty spaces created by the stretched tension of the loom.

Crafting Techniques

KNITTING

I admit I am not the most proficient knitter: I can stitch in knit and purl, but my dyscalculia prevents me from doing anything more complex than a scarf or blanket, if it requires complex pattern counting. However, I have inherited a pair of handmade oak knitting needles from my mother's grandmother which are perfect for chunky yarns, and they are my go-to tools for knitting with wild yarn. Handspun chunky yarn responds well to stocking (stockinette), moss and herringbone stitches, but note that with herringbone you will use significantly more yarn due to the additional layering on the crossover stitch. Large-scale cabling looks magnificent in a beautiful handspun. Special thanks to Marina Skua and Francesca Cluney for creating knit samples for inclusion in this book.

WEAVING

Weaving is the main outcome of my craft and textile practice. The feeling of weaving with yarn I have spun myself is deeply gratifying from a neurodiverse perspective, and creatively very satisfying in embodying the whole process of wool work. I find my outcomes are more in line with my overall vision for my weaving, and that I get a significantly more powerful response when I reflect on what I have created.

CROCHET

The crochet samples included in *Wild Yarn* were made by Bizz Fretty and Francesca Cluney, and include basic crochet stitches, Tunisian and cable stitches. The loops and chains of crochet, and the time-honoured granny square, are excellent ways to sample your handspun yarns for a larger project. Renowned British weaver Theo Moorman herself suggested creating a yarn consisting of thread constructed by a crochet chain – 'a crochet chain makes yet another interesting textured weft' – and in this way, you can create another iteration of wild yarn in and of itself! This interplay and experimentation of method, material and outcomes is a wonderful moment of spontaneity in your crafts practice, as you see what is possible.

NÅLBINDING

Nålbinding, or needle binding, is an ancient textile technique using a wood, bone or antler needle to create loops to form a textile, often shaped for a hat or sock. In a contemporary context, we can think of the technique of nålbinding as a hybrid of single-needle knitting and crochet. Historic nålbinding artefacts have been found in the ancient Jordan desert, Egypt, Peru, Scandinavia, Denmark and lands with Viking contact. As a method for use with handspun wild yarn, it works very well, from the looped nature of construction and the control over tension, to the need to join in yarn lengths, for which the spliced method of joining works is ideal (see page 112). The use of extra-wide or chunky yarn is limited only by the size of the needle's eye. However, many handmade wooden needles can be sourced which can accommodate wild yarn, not least those lovingly made by the historical reproduction craft community.

FELTING

Felting can be done with a carded batt of any thickness (if you need an outer skin adding to a pre-felted piece, for example, a very thin batt can be created), or with a thicker raw fleece. Indeed, it is becoming more usual to see felted sheepskin rugs, created as a way to make use of the whole fleece and its natural character without the need to also take the skin; the upper side looks just like a traditional sheepskin, but the reverse is comprised of a thick felted mat to hold the locks in place. (For further research, look at the work of The Living Rug Company.)

WET FELTING This requires soap, water and friction as provided by the maker. The action of rolling and pressing the wet soapy wool allows the scales on the hairs to tangle and mat together, creating a bonded textile. Whenever excess heat or cold is applied most usually to wool and animal fibres, it 'shocks' the fibres, and this refers to the rapid expansion or contraction of the fibre, resulting in structural changes, i.e. bonding and shrinkage, also known as *fulling*. I spend plenty of time as a weaver avoiding shrinking wool by mistake, so it is incredibly liberating to enjoy the processes of wet felting and the really special results it creates. I recommend an olive-oil soap for wet felting; I like to rinse my finished work with distilled water and a witch-hazel infusion, which removes the excess soap and conditions the fibres.

DRY FELTING This is a dry process that uses special sets of hooked needles to mat the fibres together, and for this reason it is also known as *needle felting*. It requires a protective surface to work on to that has a foam or spongy quality to take the impact of the needles, as well as some mindful finger protection (the barbed hooks are very similar in severity to the blade at the tip of a leather needle). Dry needle felting gives a slightly different finish to wet felting, and indeed, once a section of wet felting is dry, needle felting can be used to add some detail and definition into the work as needed.

NUNO FELTING This is the term used when wool is (wet) felted into a pre-woven textile, and this method of using a structure to hold and secure felted layers allows greater possibilities for your creative needs.

For further research, search out the felted works of Galdys Paulus, Maggie Scott, Moira Bateman and Yuli Somme.

RUG HOOK AND PILE KNOTWORK

There are many traditional and cultural methods of creating pile surfaces and knotting rugs, including the Finnish *rya*, Turkish *Ghiordes*, Persian *Senneh,* and Greek *Flokati*, plus adjacent rug-making methodologies such as proddy (*proggy* or *peg*), ribbon, latch hook, and the more recent popularity of the industrial tufting gun, as well as vintage manual tufting tools. Tufting tools, including tufting guns, are limited by the size of their eye or orifice, and are often not able to accommodate thick or variegated yarns. Some of these tools and techniques create a looped pile that is intended to either remain looped or to be cut to form a cut–pile surface.

For further research, see the pile-textile and rug-punched artworks of Finnish artist Hanna-Kaisa Korolainen and Welsh-Ghanaian artist Anya Paintsil, and the Persian knotted rugs of Shorsh Saleh.

LARK'S HEAD KNOT RUG

Knotted rug hooking is a craft I enjoy immensely. Here, I'm going to specifically speak about my improvisation, and combination of methods, tools and ground fabrics to work knotted pile surfaces within my wild-yarn textile practice. I have a simple hooked-knot method that can be used on a base cloth such as hessian sacking, wide monks cloth and open-weave handwoven textiles. I also use it to make a rya-inspired yarn that is technically a pile yarn, sometimes called feather or eyelash yarn.

TOOLS A metal rug-hook with a notch large enough to accommodate thicker yarn, or a medium crochet hook.

THE LARK'S HEAD KNOT Sometimes known as the cow hitch knot, this is a simple looped knot creating twin-tails. It is looped around a foundation yarn by hand or by tool, as during weaving or macramé; or it can be looped through an open-weave textile, such as hessian sacking or monks cloth, with the use of a rug-hook tool to create a pile texture. This pile can be cut close to the ground cloth, or left longer with organic soft-pulled tips – both methods (and those in between) have been used across cultures and craft traditions at different times.

PREPARING THE YARN The creation of wild yarn in my methodology is to be mindful of scissors, and *avoid* them where possible (blunt-cut fibres will always seek to stick out). Instead, I gently unspin a small section of yarn and pull the fibres apart, in place of directly cutting the yarn. Because I won't be trimming down the pile, the tips will be natural and variegated, and as such, will be differing lengths. I select my yarn sections and separate them free-hand, without measuring, as this creates the organic effect I am seeking to amplify. If you are concerned about the stability or delicacy of the unspun yarn once it's been separated, you can lightly dampen the tips and let them dry to bring the fibres back together. This would work if you are pulling yarn in batches; however, I mainly pull from the skein or ball as I go, and might have several shades to select from, so I tend to pull one knot's worth of yarn at a time, and lightly spray down the whole work once it is complete.

FORMING THE KNOT Loosely fold the length of yarn in half, so that the tightest spin is at the looped fold (you can add in or re-twist with your fingers at this step). Pass your rug-hook tool under the foundation thread that you will be securing the yarn onto on your base cloth; catch the curve of your folded yarn with the hook, gently pulling back beneath the base cloth thread, the way you came in. The lark's head can now be formed in one of two ways: either put down the hook and use your fingers to reach through the loop and pull the tails through to secure; or, using the hook, reach around both tails and, with a rolling motion, wrap them around the tip of the hook and pull through the loop of your yarn, tightening it by hand to the required tension.

KNOTTED PILE YARN

The lark's head knot can be used to knot strands of handspun yarn to a foundation yarn to create meterage. This makes an interesting yarn to craft with, and the pile-tails can be pushed to the right side at the end of a project to create a densely piled surface. As your work is handled more during the making process, it will naturally become slightly felted and create a unique texture based on the fibres you have blended in the original spin.

Joining Yarn: Wet Splicing or the Invisible Join

Known by many knitters as 'spit-and-splice', this technique of invisible-joining can be employed simply with a small bowl of water to hand during many of the processes in the creation of wild yarn. To join yarn, as with joining-in fibre during spinning, take the last 5cm (2in) of the working end of the yarn and split it evenly, laying in the new yarn end between the two open splices. Ensure the ends are not blunt-cut, rather pulled and soft to allow the fibres to joint and semi-felt together, forming an invisible join. Add a few drops of water and roll the section to be spliced between your palms to encourage felting.

Rag Yarn

Scrap-pieced textiles and rag yarns are found in heritage techniques that can be evidenced throughout the 1700s and 1800s, as a regular resource in making household quilts, cushions and mats; and rag collecting forms part of the traditional rag-and-bone trades of ethnic Romani and Travellers of the same era. Once outfits made from expensive milled fabrics had been worn, mended and eventually worn through, 'rags' were created to make use of every scrap and valuable strip of cloth. Clothing and sheets were stripped down into useable sections, and smaller irregular segments could be put towards patchwork and English paper-piecing work. In this regard, the textile samples used in the creation of salvaged rag-and-pieced textiles show the popular colours, patterns and textures of earlier eras, as those fabrics that were once the height of fashion became scrap over perhaps several decades. For example, a Victorian rag rug from 1880 may be employing fabric scraps from the 1840s and 1850s, and often once these artefacts themselves start to fall apart, the true colours are revealed by looking inside the seams. For heritage cultural patchworks in North America, see the Gee's Bend quilting tradition, and for more contemporary patchwork techniques research the work of designer Lu Flux.

MAKING RAG YARN

The principle of making rag yarn is to tear or cut lengths of workable fabric strips from your base fabric, with the most effective choices being woven meterage (knitted jersey will ladder and unravel, so is not suitable for this particular technique unless pre-felted), or larger pieces of vintage textile. Strips can be as short as 10cm (4in) and joined as described later in this process.

If you are using vintage fabric, I recommend you prewash the whole textile piece on a warm wash to clean and preshrink *before* you make it into a yarn that will go on to become something else, to minimize the potential for future shrinkage. Also, it's sometimes the case that vintage fabrics will not survive the wash and will disintegrate or develop large holes. This is because in the early days of dry-cleaning, the solvent soaks used to impregnate the fabrics would essentially rot the structural integrity of the cloth over time, so it's good to edit these out before doing all the hard work of making your rag yarn.

At the prewash stage, this would also be a good moment to dye your fabric if you are planning on doing that. The finished rag yarn can also be dyed by either dipping or full submersion, and this allows for an ombré along the hank, or ikat-inspired painted lengths, traditionally used for warps. The word 'ikat' comes from the Indonesian word for 'tie' and true cultural ikat uses a thread-resist technique, which includes wrapping the yarn in sections before dyeing/painting. We can see the adaptation of the principles of ikat within both vintage and contemporary tie-dye techniques that use thread-wrapping as a dye-pattern resist.

PREPARING THE FABRIC STRIPS

There is a wonderfully simple way to find a cloth's straight-grain and reduce the use of active cutting by tearing your fabric strips. This method doesn't work for every single fabric, and while it won't work on velvet or densely pattern-woven or brocade fabrics, it will work for the majority of tabby weaves.

Assess the fabric width and length, and take account of any print direction to get the best out of your material. Whether you choose long or short strips, you may add or reduce the texture based on the number of joining sections to add moments of bulk and texture: i.e. shorter sections = more joins = more texture.

Beginning at an edge of your material, take snips or scissors and make an initial short cut of about 2cm (¾in) deep. We are here creating a true straight grain and so the cut away might be discarded if it is from an old cut or non-straight edge (curved or bias edges will fray and not create a stable yarn).

From your now true straight edge, decide how wide you would like your strip to be: this might be from around 3cm (1⅛in) up to 30cm (12in) depending on your needs: narrow strips = longer meterage of your finished yarn.

Once you decide on your strip width, make a 2cm (¾in) snip in the correct place parallel to your true straight grain; then, holding each side of the cut in opposite hands, and with a strong and committed force, pull the two sides apart to the full extent of your arms. This will create a dramatic ripping sound, and it will provide you with a perfectly straight edge, and that edge will have a lovely soft and feathered finish. You may also get single stray threads from each tear. Gather these waste fibres up as you go and keep them for other projects; indeed, you can card these into a future yarn blend.

JOINING FABRIC STRIPS

Fold the end of a strip over with about a 3cm (1⅛in) depth, take your scissors and carefully cut into the centre of the fold by around 1cm (⅜in).

Open the fold, and thread the end of a new strip through the cut.

Repeat the fold-and-cut technique with the newly threaded end, then thread the uncut end of the new strip through the newly made cut (this is all happening on the new strip).

Gently pull the new strip through itself until it starts to tighten around the previous end; pull firmly here, as the two ends create a join that resembles a knot.

You can experiment here with leaving a longer tail for extra texture (this can be done by folding extra fabric over at the fold-and-cut step).

Keep going until all your strips are joined: this rag yarn can be used as it is, rolled up into a ball or wound into hanks on the niddy-noddy.

Additionally, rag yarn lengths can be spun in the same way other fibres are spun, on a spindle or wheel (and subsequently plied), so in this regard you can consider it as rag-roving. If it is to be spun, then it will need to be soaked and weighted in the same way as other spun fibres, as the energy put into the twist will need to be set and balanced.

Any small rag strips and scrap offcuts that didn't make the finished yarn can be shredded down and included in future batts, or used as knotted tufts around the rya-inspired pile rug.

A Wild Yarn Sampler

In the honoured tradition of needlework, I invite a project to finish the guidance of my book by creating a sampler from the yarn you have spun.

Howsoever you choose to craft in practice, creating a work from a collection of smaller elements and experimental yarns will build up a work that is an entire and complete study for you to review, assess and reflect upon as a step towards the next work you make.

What might you glean from the materials, structure and overall effect in combinations? More importantly, how does it make you feel? How do you receive your own work artistically, emotionally? How well do you recognize your voice and signature in the yarns you have spun? This is storytelling.

In this way, the creation of a sampler is a testimony to newly embodied skills and the curve of learning a new set of techniques.

Reflection

In summary and in closing *Wild Yarn*, I'm reminded of all the makers that have gone before us, to whom we owe an enormous debt of gratitude, not just for their innovations, revivals, experiments and practical research, but for their communication and mentorship of craft. The spirit of teaching craft, which is the honouring of wisdom, the translation of techniques and the sharing of knowledge, must continue to flow as a river into the future of humanity. Thankfully, this feels like a natural impulse of a creative life, to disseminate craft organically, thereby propagating the safeguarding of a living continuum.

I found the voices of the craftswomen who have gone before me, many before my lifetime, exceptionally timely, comforting and ever present. Their challenges are our challenges: time has not altered this fact, only they have gone ahead, and if we are lucky, we have their wisdom and teachings preserved in our books and hands. As with all things, the recorded writing of women is not so ancient, although our work of creation is the original great work. We cannot fail to feel a sense of familiarity and comfort when we read the words of craftswomen, as those quoted in this book: Theo Moorman, Anni Albers, Virginia Woolf, Georgia O'Keeffe, et al… or view their works in the form they took, be it poetry, painting, textile. Craftspeople recognize the Craft in others, as expressed in their works. So, from this position, we can look both forwards and backwards to affirm the consistency of the path as it cycles back to us in the present moment:

'It is interesting to see how many young people, faced with the great world problems of pollution, unbalance of natural forces, even stark threats of annihilation, are turning to producing, by the simplest of means, the basic necessities of existence. In addition to the building of huts and shelters and the growing of food, some of these young people are spinning, weaving and knitting their own garments and blankets from natural materials with a most honest urgency, quite divorced from any theoretical or idealistic plans to put the clock back. As Noah, hearing and seeing the waters rising, must have recognized the power put into his hands in the form of the simplest possible tools and materials, the hammers, nails, and planks of wood which were to save the living world, so perhaps spinners and weavers today treasure and revere their spinning wheels, looms, and fleeces when they hear the daily news that pours from radio and television.'

Theo Moorman,
Weaving as an Art Form

Bibliography

Abakanowicz, Magdalena, *Magdalena Abakanowicz*, 2022, Tate

Albers, Anni, *On Weaving*, 1965, Princeton University Press

Albers, Anni, *On Designing*, 1943, Wesleyan University Press

Alexander, Christopher, *A Foreshadowing of 21st Century Art, The Color and Geometry of Very Early Turkish Carpets (Center for Environmental Structure, Vol 7)*, 1993, Oxford University Press

Bachelard, Gaston, *The Poetics of Space*, 1957, Presses Universitaries de France

Baines, Patricia, *Linen: Hand Spinning and Weaving, 1989*, Batsford

Baines, Patricia, *Spinning Wheels, Spinners & Spinning*, 1977, Batsford

Banfield Jill, & Cook-Wallace, Hanna, Lecture 17; *Pearls and Other Organic Gems*, UC Berkeley, 2002, https://nature.berkeley.edu/classes/eps2/wisc/Lect17.html

Beggs, Michael, Thomson, Julie J., *Weaving at Black Mountain College*, 2023, Black Mountain College Museum/Yale University Press

Beutlich, Tadek, *The Technique of Woven Tapestry*, 1986, Batsford

Bourgeois, Louise, *The Woven Child*, 2022, Hayward Gallery/Hatje Cantz

Bright Moon, Imogen, *The Selkie Weaving: & The Wild Feminine*, 2018, Magpie

Bright Moon, Imogen, *Black Tent / Black Sarah*, 2022, Bright Moon Press

Byram, Jennifer, *Many Makers: Collaborative Renewal of Chahta Nan Tvnna (Choctaw Textiles)*, Journal of Textile Design Research and Practice, Volume 9, 2021, The Textile Society of America.

Chislett, Helen & Linley, David, *Craft Britain: Why Making Matters*, 2022, OH Editions

Christiansen, Carol, *Taatit Rugs: The Pile Bedcovers of Shetland*, 2015, Shetland Heritage

Clark, Ann Nolan, *Little Herder in Autumn*, 1988, Ancient City Press

Collingwood, Peter, *The Techniques of Rug Weaving*, 1968, Faber & Faber

Collingwood, Peter, *The Maker's Hand*, 1987, Lark/Interweave

De Amaral, Olga, *To Weave a Rock*, 2020, arnoldsche/Museum of Fine Arts, Houston

Diaper, Hilary, *Theo Moorman 1907–1990: Her Life and Work as an Artist Weaver*, 1992, University Gallery Leeds

Edwards, Jilly, *Joy: Yellow is the New Blue*, 2017, Colophon

Edwards, Jilly, *Yellows & Pinks*, 2021

Fox, Alice, *Wild Textiles: Grown, Foraged, Found*, 2022, Batsford

Franquemont, Abby, *Respect the Spindle*, 2009, Interweave

Frayling, Christopher, *On Craftsmanship: Towards a New Bauhaus*, 2011, Oberon

Goldsworthy, Andy, *Stone*, 1994, Viking

Gustafson, Heidi, *Book of Earth*, 2023, Abrams

Gustafson, Paula, *Salish Weaving*, 1980, Douglas & McIntyre

Hicks, Sheila, *Material Voices*, 2016, Joslyn Art Museum

Hicks, Sheila, *Weaving as Metaphor*, 2006, Bard

Hillyer, Carolyn, *Weaver's Oracle*, 2016, Seventh Wave

Kirke, Betty, *Madeleine Vionnet*, 2005, Chronicle Books

Kirkham, Pat, *Harry Peach: Dryad and the DIA*, 1986, The Design Council

Knitting Dragonflies, http://knittingdragonflies.blogspot.com/2008/11/review-of-kick-spindles-or-mother.html, 2008

Langlands, Alexander, *CRÆFT*, 2017, Faber & Faber

Martin, Agnes, *The Distillation of Color*, 2021, Pace

Mason, Jessica, *Spinning, Heart & Hand, 2017*, Bezalel Workshops Booklet

MccGwire, Kate, *Kate MccGwire*, Anomie Publishing

Moorman, Theo, *Weaving as an Art Form*, 1975, Schiffer Publishing

Myserson, Jeremy, *Makepeace: A Spirit of Adventure in Craft & Design*, 1995, Conran Octopus

O'Keeffe, Georgia, *Some Memories of Drawings*, 1974, Atlantis Editions

Patterson, Karen (Editor), *Lenore Tawney: Mirror of the Universe*, 1975, University of Chicago Press

Peach, Harry, Craftsmen All: An Anthology, 1948, Dryad Press

Reichard, Gladys, *Spider Woman: A Story of Navajo Weavers and Chanters*, 1934, University of New Mexico Press.

Robson, Deborah & Ekarius, Carol, *The Fleece & Fiber Sourcebook*, 2011, Storey

Ross, Mabel, *Encyclopedia of Handspinning*, 1988, Batsford

Rothko, Christopher & Bishop, Janet, *Rothko: The Color Field Paintings*, 2016, Chronicle Books

Smart, Pamela, *Rothko Chapel: An Oasis for Reflection*, 2021, Rizzoli Electa

Teal, Peter, *Hand Woolcombing and Spinning*, 1976, Blandford

Teller Pete, Lynda & Teller Ornelas, Barbara, *Spider Woman's Children: Navajo Weavers Today*, 2018, Thrums

Teller Pete, Lynda & Teller Ornelas, Barbara, *How to Weave a Navajo Rug: And Other Lessons from Spider Woman*, 2020, Thrums

Treggiden, Katie, *Weaving: Contemporary Makers on the Loom*, 2018, Ludion

Wayland Barber, Elizabeth, *Women's Work: The First 20,000 Years – Women, Cloth and Society in Early Times*, 1994, W.W.Norton

Weiner, Ann & Schneider, Jane, *Cloth and Human Experience*, 1989, Smithsonian

Wilkes, Stephany, *Raw Materials: Working Wool in the West*, 2018, Oregon State University Press

Willcox, Donald, *Techniques of Rya Knotting*, 1971, Van Nostrand Reinhold

Wissa Wassef, Ramses, *Woven by Hand*, 1972, Hamlyn

Woolf, Virginia, *Liberty*, 2017, Vintage

Artists & Organisations

Anya Paintsil

Association of Guilds of Weavers, Spinners and Dyers

Bonsai Woman

Caravane Earth

Choctaw Cultural Center

Craft in America

Crafts Council Makers Directory

Cynthia Alberto

Evelyn Vanderhoop

Ghazala Collective

Gladys Paulus

Hanna–Kaisa Korolainen

Heritage Crafts Makers Directory

Homo Faber Guide, Michelangelo Foundation

Institute of Nomadic Architecture

Jessica Mason

Jilly Edwards

Knitting Dragonflies

Lily Hope

Loewe Craft Prize

Maggie Scott

Marina Skua

Moira Bateman

Navajo Cultural Arts

Rachel Scott

Sally Pointer

Shorsh Saleh

TahNibaa Naataanii

The Nettle Dress Film (Allan Brown and Dylan Howitt)

V&A Collections Online

Will Cruikshank

Zefren-M (Ephraim Anderson)

Resources: Fibre & Tool Suppliers

Ashford: fibre and tool supplier.

Bodrighy Wood: variety of spindle types.

Dunelm Turning: variety of heritage and cultural spindles and spinning bowls.

Fernhill Fibre: fibre and tool supplier.

Fibre Hut: fibre and tool supplier.

George Weil: fibre and tool supplier.

Highland Colours: traditionally dyed fibres and yarn by Sarah Matthess.

Isle of Auskerry: Teresa Probert's heritage flock of North Ronaldsay sheep, Orkney.

I-Spin: 3D printed spinner adaptations for domestic sewing machines.

IST Crafts: spindles of all kinds.

Lauriston Farm: biodynanic North Ronaldsay yarn production.

Liberty: specialist haberdashery department.

Living Past UK: fired-clay loom weights, used to weight yarn.

Loop London: specialist yarn shop.

Marina Skua: hand spinning, dyeing and knitting.

Overthrow Riddles & Sieves: handmade wool-washing tools.

Spindle & Skein: hand spinning, dyeing and crafts by Annabelle Cornell.

The Living Rug Company: fibre and tool supplier.

The Natural Fibre Company: organic-standard wool processing for small batch producers.

True Creations Woodturning (USA): portable kick spindles.

Wingham Wool Work: fibre suppliers and tool makers.

World of Wool: fibre and tool supplier.

YAK: independent yarn and knitting shop in Brighton.

Yarn Yarn: ethically sourced yarns including wild silks, nettle, recycled sari silk yarns and newspaper yarns.

Acknowledgements

My deepest thanks to Frida Green, Nicola Newman, Rebecca Armstrong and the Batsford Books team, and photographers extraordinaire Béla Váradi, Michaela Meadow and Alun Callender. To my mother Sally, cousins Gem Hall, Lisa Smith, Sarah Edwards, Cas Holmes, Dee and Dolly Cooper, Rima Staines and Jo Clement for your consistent love, creativity and Romani solidarity. Teresa Probert and Hamish Auskerry for all the wonderful wool and stories from your island. Daniel Carpenter, Mary Lewis and my colleagues at Heritage Crafts for your support. Bizz Fretty, Francesca Cluney, Xen Calviou, and Marina Skua for your expert samples for this book and consistent kindness, thank you. Paul Martin for the love and care you gave me during the art therapy years. Phoebe Cummings, Wilma Woolf, Holly Ringland for your powerful visions, voices, and works. Elaine Shepard Bolt for collaborations in Moominland; to Maarit Kalmakuri for being my fashion-workshop best friend since 2001. Weaving solidarity with Jilly Edwards and Catarina Riccabona; much respect to Hanna-Kaisa Korolainen and Gladys Paulus for your inspirational artworks. Thank you to Molly Bray, Allan Brown, Jessica Mason and Christabel Balfour for craft support on the journey during the early days. Blessings to Kristin Perers and Bluebell for a glorious day talking colours and symbols in the spirit. Thank you to Rafaela Ricardo, Natalie Melton and all my colleagues on the EAC at Crafts Council; to Rose Sinclair MBE for your support and friendship. Kathy Lacour, Sarah Myerscough at the creative team at The New Craftsmen. Victoria Bradley at the V&A Museum for your support, good conversations and mutual respect for the work of Theo Moorman. To my dearest Rose Riedel O'Brien and Lily Aisbitt–Waugh for walking this path of craft with me, in love. To my dear friend Melody Vaughan for your honest friendship and enduring kindness over the years, thank you. Special thanks to Pam Hutley in Australia for your care and support, weaver-to-weaver. And to all the young spinners to come, starting with Finn, Oscar, Orson, Emrys, Izzy, Chloe, Carlos, Lexi, Isobel and Louis: may you all grow in craft and share with friends, and teach your own children, one day.

In gratitude, Imogen

In memoriam,
Vivienne Westwood,
1941-2022

First published in the United Kingdom

in 2024 by

Batsford

43 Great Ormond Street

London

WC1N 3HZ

An imprint of B. T. Batsford Holdings Limited

Photography by Béla Váradi, Michaela Meadow and Alun Callender

ISBN 9781849949019

A CIP catalogue record for this book is available from the British Library.

10 9 8 7 6 5 4 3 2 1

Reproduction by Rival Colour Ltd, UK

Printed and bound by Toppan Leefung Printing International, Ltd

This book can be ordered direct from the publisher at www.batsfordbooks.com, or try your local bookshop.